The Road to Freedom

The Road to Freedom

✦

A Study Guide to Chimamanda Ngozi Adichie's Purple Hibiscus

Daniela Muscat &
Stephanie Xerri Agius

iUniverse, Inc.
New York   Bloomington

The Road to Freedom
A Study Guide to Chimamanda Ngozi
Adichie's 'Purple Hibiscus'

Front cover illustration by Betty Gerstner

iUniverse books may be ordered through booksellers or by contacting:

*iUniverse
1663 Liberty Drive
Bloomington, IN 47403
www.iuniverse.com
1-800-Authors (1-800-288-4677)*

*Because of the dynamic nature of the Internet, any Web addresses or
links contained in this book may have changed since publication and may
no longer be valid.*

*ISBN: 978-1-4401-8976-0 (sc)
ISBN: 978-1-4401-8978-4 (ebk)*

Printed in the United States of America

iUniverse rev. date: 01/18/2010

Contents

About the author

Chimamanda Ngozi Adichie was born in September 1977 in Abba, Nigeria. Adichie grew up in Nigeria and has always been very interested in the idea of ethnicity. She was educated in Nigeria and then went on to further her studies at various American universities in Philadelphia, Connecticut and Baltimore. Adichie's parents both worked at the University of Nsukka and so Adichie is well-acquainted with this setting as well as with university life in America.

Adichie also greatly admires the works of Chinua Achebe, a world-renowned Nigerian author. Indeed her favourite book is *Arrow of God* by Chinua Achebe. Adichie used to love writing for her family from a very early age and she remains a very prolific and varied writer as she has written short stories, novels, articles and journals.

Adichie published her first novel *Purple Hibiscus*, in 2003, a novel which received much attention as well as acclaim. Adichie's second novel was *Half of a Yellow Sun* (2006), for which she was awarded the Orange Broadband Prize for Fiction in 2007, is set during the Biafran war. Adichie has also won and been short-listed for many prestigious prizes such as the Hurston/Wright Legacy Award in 2004 and the Commonwealth Writers' Prize in 2005 for her first novel *Purple Hibiscus*.

The Plot

Set in Enugu, Nigeria, on the eve of a military coup, *Purple Hibiscus* tells the story of fifteen-year-old Kambili and her painful awakening from an abusive home life to the beginnings of personal freedom. Kambili and her brother Jaja grow up under their father's watchful eye and wrathful anger. Their father is a fanatically religious man and demands perfection from his children— at school, at home, and in their religious devotion. Any infraction, however slight, is met with physical punishment, from beatings and whippings to having boiling water poured over their feet. He beats his wife so badly that she suffers a miscarriage. It is this stifling and fear-drenched environment that shapes Kambili and makes her so shy she can barely speak, so timid she doesn't know the sound of her own laughter.

When Kambili and Jaja go to visit their high-spirited Aunty Ifeoma, a university professor at Nsukka University, their world becomes suddenly larger, louder, richer, and freer. Here Kambili is plunged into a world where children and adults alike say what they think without fear, and everyone can laugh, argue, question, and challenge each other openly. Though Aunty Ifeoma is Catholic, she still embraces traditional African songs and beliefs, and her loving approach to life is a warm and welcome change from the rigid atmosphere of Kambili's home. Immersed in this new world, Kambili begins to discover her own voice, her ability to laugh and to make others laugh. She also begins to fall in love with a charismatic young priest who helps her to see her own worth, clearly, for the first time.

KOGI

BENUE

EDO

ANAMBRA

Enugu

RIA

CROSS
RIVER

CAMEROON

DELTA   IMO

ABIA

AKWA
IBOM

The violence of Kambili's home life is echoed in Nigeria, as a repressive regime takes power in a military coup. Her father's newspaper is under pressure from the new government, the lecturers have gone on strike at the university where Aunty Ifeoma teaches, and corruption runs rampant throughout the country. It is a time of great turmoil, both personal and political, and the lives of all the main characters are brought to crisis points. In this beautifully written and poignant first novel, Chimamanda Ngozi Adichie offers a moving and nuanced exploration of the ongoing tension between the forces of oppression and the irrepressible human desire to be free.

Purple Hibiscus: A note about the novel's sequence

The novel is divided into four sections and hence the timeline is not linear. It begins with an incident that catapults Kambili's family into troubled conflicts between the members of the family (Palm Sunday). The section that follows takes the reader to the events preceding those of the first section, so that one understands the opening scene in its entirety and thus starts piecing the novel together (Before Palm Sunday).

The third section is the aftermath of the events underlining Palm Sunday (After Palm Sunday) and this neatly blends into the final section, which serves as an epilogue, 'A Different Silence – The Present'. The logic or purpose behind such a structuring of the novel is to reflect and thus emphasise the chaos that is shaping the lives of Kambili and her family as well as the other Nigerian people who are experiencing yet another coup d'etat – the confusion in the political and urban scenery is rampant, democracy is but a farce, students are rioting outside the university, and people are dragged into the streets and hacked to death in front of their relatives.

Meanwhile, Kambili is going through the turmoil of adolescence and her brother Jaja is undergoing a radical change in character; even though their daily problems may seem insignificant compared to those who are actually dying or losing their homes and jobs, Adichie manages to give their story the weight it deserves. Moreover, since it is told from Kambili's perspective, the latter encompasses and takes in all that is going on around her, thus giving justice to the injustices she is aware of.

The Title

In the novel by Adichie, the title *Purple Hibiscus* conceals a symbolic meaning. In the town where Kambili and her family live, Enugu, Kambili notes that it is uncommon to find the purple hibiscus; theirs, in fact, is red. On the other hand, when Kambili and her brother Jaja visit Aunty Ifeoma and her children in a poorer town, Nsukka, they are amazed by the beauty of the flower's strong purple hue. Later, Kambili and Jaja are given a graft of the flower so they too can have a purple rather than a mere red hibiscus. In the house of Aunty Ifeoma, she and her children are free to speak their mind and laugh, notwithstanding the poverty they have to endure daily. On the contrary, in Kambili's house this behaviour is considered disdainful by their father, hence the purple hibiscus represents the freedom, happiness and strength-of-character that Kambili and Jaja crave. The act of trying to grow the purple hibiscus back in Enugu outside their home symbolises their inner desire to be like Ifeoma's children in mind and spirit. The relevance of this episode to the title of the novel, together with other events and characters' actions laid down by Adichie, brings the reader to ponder on the symbolic meaning of the colour and hence the meaning of the title.

Breaking Gods – Palm Sunday

Synopsis – section 1 (pages 3 to 16)

Eugene and his family go to Sunday mass and he is highly praised during mass by Father Benedict, the parish priest, for his many qualities especially his generosity. Jaja does not receive communion during mass and this results in a clash developing between Eugene and his son once they get home. Eugene demands to know why Jaja has not received communion, since he usually informs Father Benedict about people who skip communion. Jaja confronts his father and says that if not receiving "the wafer" is death then he wants to die. Eugene throws the missal at Jaja, misses and hits the figurines. Beatrice, Eugene's wife, comes in and picks up the smashed figurines in silence. Beatrice pretends that the figurines are unimportant even though whenever she would have received a swollen eye she would go downstairs to polish the figurines.

They soon meet for lunch and Eugene prays for twenty minutes before the meal. Eugene brings in some cashew juice which is one of his new products and they all praise it except Jaja. Eugene demands that Jaja says something and so Jaja says thanks and leaves the table before Eugene has prayed after the meal.

Kambili develops a cough and stays in bed at dinner time and so Beatrice and Eugene come to see her and she learns that Jaja has not come down for dinner. Kambili thinks of Aunty Ifeoma's purple hibiscus and of breaking the silence.

Analysis – section 1 (pages 3 to 16)

The first section is aptly entitled 'Breaking Gods' as it is in this section that one is presented with a clash between Eugene and Jaja, two characters who have been at odds with each other for a while. The novel starts with a reference to Chinua Achebe's *Things Fall Apart* and this alludes to how things will definitely change in the Achike household now that Jaja has broken the silence and stood up to his father.

The reader is also immediately acquainted with Eugene's violent reactions towards his son's lack of observation of religious routines and how this is simply not tolerated by Eugene. However Eugene's behaviour changes drastically outside the home. In the public eye, he is considered to be a very altruistic man whilst being a staunch Catholic and a fervent follower of Western ways who has renounced the traditional Igbo religion.

It is at this stage in the narrative that Jaja has finally plucked up the courage to stand up to his controlling father and to oppose what Eugene holds dear. Therefore, Jaja seeks to antagonise Eugene by refraining from receiving communion and by referring to the host as "the wafer". Notwithstanding the conflict that develops between father and son, Beatrice does not mention Jaja's rebellion and she keeps quiet throughout.

Kambili, Eugene's daughter, who is but fifteen years old, narrates *Purple Hibiscus* and thus the novel focuses more on the family rather than the political and social situation in Nigeria. Kambili describes how Father Benedict praises Eugene since he gives generous donations to the church and thus Father Benedict sings Eugene's praises during his sermons. Eugene also holds Father Benedict in high regard since he shies away from what is traditional and Nigerian and he tries to impose Western ways instead.

Once they get home Eugene is furious that Jaja persists in disobeying him and by his disrespectful description of the host as "the wafer". Eugene's reaction is to fling the missal at Jaja and this is a potent symbol of how Eugene's particular interpretation of religion leads him to violence. The missal does not hit Jaja as Eugene had intended, but it breaks Beatrice's figurines instead. Beatrice used to spend time polishing these figurines after she would have suffered violence at Eugene's hand and so the breaking of the figurines implies that things have definitely changed in the Achike household.

They soon sit down to tea and Eugene usually gives his children a "love sip" from his tea. Kambili does not enjoy this as the tea is hot but no one dares to argue with Eugene for fear of making him angry. After tea, Kambili looks out from her bedroom window and remembers when government agents had come to see Eugene. Jaja had mentioned that their car was full of foreign money which shows that corruption runs rampant in Nigeria.

As they gather for lunch the tension at the dinner table is immediately apparent as both Kambili and Beatrice know that Jaja will be punished and they try to avert Jaja's punishment. However Jaja continues to antagonise Eugene by means of his behaviour at table and by choosing to leave the table early. Kambili is so worried about Eugene's reaction to Jaja's rebellion that she becomes physically ill. However what Jaja has done is to assert himself to his controlling father and his defiance shows that he is in search of freedom and this is associated with Aunty Ifeoma and her purple hibiscus.

Speaking with our spirits – Before Palm Sunday

Synopsis – section 2 – chapter 1 (pages 19 to 26)

Beatrice tells Kambili that she is pregnant and that she has had miscarriages before and the village people had sent their daughters to Eugene to have children with but Eugene had refused to take a second wife. The members of the Miraculous Medal prayer group come to visit and Beatrice gives them the food she has prepared as usual. Jaja comes into Kambili's room and she tells him about Beatrice being pregnant.

The coup is announced over the radio and Eugene phones his editor Ade Coker to cover the story. The Achike family spends their Sunday quietly reading the major newspapers. The *Standard* is Eugene's paper and it seems like the most objective newspaper, whilst some papers such as *Nigeria Today* praise the coming to power of the military general.

Analysis – section 2 – chapter 1 (pages 19 to 26)

The second section of the novel goes on to describe what happened before the events that took place in the first section. One of the striking features about the daily routine of the

Achike family is that Eugene controls what his children do since they are obliged to follow a timetable that he has drawn up.

When Beatrice tells Kambili that she is pregnant, one can appreciate how important the issue of fertility is in this culture, so much so that the villagers send their daughters for Eugene to take as a second wife and thus give him more children after the news about Beatrice's miscarriages had spread. However Eugene does not opt for a second wife since this goes against Catholic beliefs and Kambili admires Eugene for this.

Life in the Achike household is also very quiet as they do not communicate much and when they do, it is usually by means of a glance. Kambili and Jaja also tend to speak about issues that they already know about and it seems to be their way of opting not to speak about Eugene's violent behaviour.

The novel suddenly shifts from the familial to the political scene when a coup is announced over the radio. This implies a sudden unconstitutional overthrow of the government by power thirsty men. Eugene, who has experienced previous coups, knows that the situation will go from bad to worse as other powerful men will seek to overthrow those who are in power. He is worried about this vicious cycle and his preoccupations seem to be shared by the various newspapers the Achike family reads.

Synopsis – section 2 – chapter 2 (pages 27 to 36)

Various changes happen after the announcement of the coup. The newspapers are more reserved, people stick green branches to their cars to indicate solidarity, there are protesters in Government Square, various roadblocks are set up and armed soldiers patrol the streets.

It is Pentecost Sunday and the Achike family goes to mass where a newly ordained priest says mass. Eugene greets people as they leave the church and Beatrice asks to be left in the car as Eugene is about to go to visit Father Benedict as she feels nauseous. However she gives in and they visit Father Benedict while he is having lunch. Once they get home they eat in silence and after the meal Eugene prays for the forgiveness of the person who did not want to visit Father Benedict earlier that day.

Kambili hears noises in her parents' room after lunch and then Eugene carries Beatrice downstairs and into the car while blood trickles behind them. Jaja and Kambili clean it up and they speak about three men who were publicly executed and not about their mother. Beatrice returns the following day wearing a T-shirt with 'GOD IS LOVE' printed on it. She wears a vacant expression and she tells them that she has lost the baby. Beatrice starts to wash the figurines and hugs herself in the centre of the room. Kambili starts reading and the print turns red. Later on the family, led by Eugene, recite novenas for their mother's forgiveness.

Analysis – section 2 – chapter 2 (pages 27 to 36)

Tension continues to rise in society at large and the *Standard* seems to be the only newspaper which dares to state the facts. Notwithstanding this climate of change, life in the Achike household is the same as usual. It is Pentecost Sunday and they hear mass where the colour red is dominant. The colour has religious significance in this context. However it will become increasingly significant as Eugene becomes violent.

Once mass is over one may see how religion is of extreme importance to Eugene as he gives priority to his habitual visit to Father Benedict's than to his wife who is visibly unwell.

Upon getting home, one may see how Sundays are usually extremely quiet, however the characters are seen to bear the silence rather than to seek it.

Later in the day, Eugene makes Beatrice feel sorry for having tried to avoid visiting Father Benedict as they usually do. Eugene asks for forgiveness for Beatrice's shortcoming in front of the children and then he also punishes her physically and consequently she has to be taken to hospital.

Kambili and Jaja choose to speak about what is happening in society at large rather than to bring themselves to discuss the domestic violence that they have just witnessed. Once Beatrice is discharged from hospital the impact of what has happened is immediately apparent as Beatrice has just miscarried as a result of Eugene's violence. Beatrice ironically wears a T-shirt with 'GOD IS LOVE' printed on it and she sets to polishing the figurines which seems to be her way of dealing with the pain.

Later on, Eugene, together with the other members of the family, insists that they should pray for their mother's forgiveness. The children are baffled by this and the reader is left to ponder why Eugene insists on displacing the guilt for this loss onto his wife.

Synopsis – section 2 – chapter 3 (pages 37 to 51)

Yewande, Ade Coker's wife, comes to tell Eugene that Ade has been abducted as he was leaving the offices of the *Standard.* However, Kambili is more worried by the fact that she has come second in class. Jaja has come first in class as usual. Eugene sees Kambili's report card and asks who has come first. They have dinner and Eugene brings in a new type of biscuit for them to taste and they all praise the new product. Kambili follows Eugene to his room after dinner for her punishment, but Kambili is sent away as Eugene receives a call about Ade Coker who is soon to be released and Eugene mentions that the soldiers have tortured Ade by having put out a lot of cigarettes on his back. Eugene therefore decides that the *Standard* is going to start publishing underground.

As Kambili is being driven to school, she sees soldiers destroying some vegetable stalls and a hawker being whipped for spitting at the soldiers. Kambili attends the Daughters of the Immaculate Heart Secondary School, and Eugene goes to class with her on this particular day to tell her that she can do just as well as Chinwe Jideze. Mother Lucy leads the morning assembly during which they sing the national anthem and Kambili is chosen to say the pledge but she gets tongue-tied. Once in class Kambili speaks to Ezinne, her friend in class, whilst Chinwe Jideze tries to persuade her classmates to vote for her as class prefect. The other students call Kambili "backyard snob" since she does not socialise with others and she runs off after the last lesson.

Analysis – section 2 – chapter 3 (pages 37 to 51)

Ade Coker is abducted by the military leaders for speaking too openly about drugs and corruption in Nigeria thus showing that the military leaders limit the press' freedom to make the truth known to Nigeria's citizens. Upon hearing about this, Eugene immediately tries to free Ade Coker whilst making Kambili afraid of him since she has placed second in class. Kambili wants to make her father proud of her but she is simultaneously afraid of his reaction to the news. After eating Kambili is called to Eugene's room for her punishment and the contrast between the safety the room used to represent to her and the violence it now implies strikes Kambili as she enters the room.

However, instead of punishing Kambili, Eugene answers a phone call about Ade Coker who has been released due to Eugene's influence and generosity. Ade Coker is described as a very determined man since his detention was meant to be taken as a warning but Ade Coker continues to state the facts and be just as outspoken as he was before.

Social tension appears to be increasing as the *Standard*'s members of staff are forced to go underground in order to avoid retaliation from the military leaders. Also the incident of the woman with the vegetable stall shows that the military leaders are becoming more violent and that no one can question their deeds. Kambili's heart goes out to this oppressed woman but Kambili cannot help her in any way.

On this particular day, Eugene accompanies Kambili to class since she has placed second and this is meant to make her work harder. Eugene speaks of how he had converted to Catholicism in order to make a major change in his life, since the missionaries allowed Eugene to work as a gardener and houseboy and then to attend St Gregory's Secondary School. Thus he had received a good education and they had gained another convert to the new religion.

At school, Kambili is seen as a very shy person who often gets tongue-tied. She is very reserved and is not part of a group or "clique" at school. Indeed the other students misunderstand her reserved nature for snobbery, thus they call her "backyard snob". However, she does have a friend called Ezinne and Kambili values her friendship and is grateful for it, but nothing comes before her father's good opinion of her.

Synopsis – section 2 – chapter 4 (pages 52 to 70)

It is December and Kambili focuses on placing first in class. The Achike family along with Sisi and Kevin set off to their residence in Abba and they say the rosary on the way. They stop to buy a snack and are faced by an onslaught of hawkers. However Eugene distributes money to every hawker. Upon arriving at Abba Town people greet Eugene as *Omelora* or The One Who Does For the Community as he donates money and invites the people of the village to eat at his house. Ade Coker and his family stop by to say merry Christmas on their way to Lagos. Ade greets Jaja and Kambili and comments on how quiet they are.

Kambili and Jaja do not have to follow a schedule whilst at Abba and they can converse more. When Eugene had been given the title of *Omelora* he had invited the people of the village to a feast at his home. The children go down for morning prayers led by Eugene and that afternoon they are to meet Papa-Nnukwu for fifteen minutes. Papa-Nnukwu managed to bring about the meeting by appealing to the extended family. Eugene had offered to build Papa–Nnukwu a house, buy him a car and to hire a driver if he converted to Catholicism, but Papa-Nnukwu refused.

Kevin drives the children to Papa-Nnukwu's house and Papa-Nnukwu gives them a hearty welcome as he offers them food which they refuse. Papa-Nnukwu praises the children whilst speaking of his waning health. Aunty Ifeoma helps Papa-Nnukwu out a great deal by bringing him medicines even though she has come upon hard times since her husband died and so Ifeoma and her children cannot see Papa-Nnukwu as often as they would like to. Ifeoma and Eugene had argued since Eugene decided not to allow Papa-Nnukwu into his house and they have only recently resumed talking to one another.

Jaja says the right thing whilst they are conversing and Papa-Nnukwu praises his intelligence and he says that Jaja resembles his father in this respect. Kambili feels sorry for her grandfather since he barely has enough to eat.

Kambili notices the pagan shrine that Papa-Nnukwu has in his yard and upon receiving the small cash gift that Eugene sent him, Papa-Nnukwu shows no displeasure even though he knows that it is a small gift. Kambili thinks of how much Eugene respects Beatrice's father whom they call grandfather since he was one of the first converts to Catholicism. He had done a lot to help the missionaries at the time and he also used to quote from statements issued by the Vatican and was anglicised.

Kambili and Jaja's time with Papa-Nnukwu passes pleasantly, but they stay for twenty-five minutes rather than fifteen minutes and so Eugene tells them to pray for forgiveness when they get home. Eugene is also enraged to find that a man by the name of Anikwenwa has been allowed into his house since Anikwenwa has come to tell Eugene off for treating a man of Papa-Nnukwu's age group like this and he is led off Eugene's property.

Analysis – section 2 – chapter 4 (pages 52 – 70)

Kambili fears Eugene and his violent behaviour, thus studying and placing first in class become her priority and it is for this reason that she does not pay attention to what her peers say about her.

Christmas is approaching and thus the Achike family sets off to Abba for the holidays as they usually do. Eugene insists that his family says the rosary as they drive to Abba. When they stop for a snack he donates money to those in need.

Upon arriving at Abba, a sense of community and belonging is intensely felt and Eugene's presence in town is much appreciated especially since he is so generous to the people. The villagers address Eugene as *Omelora*, thereby stressing his altruism. Eugene is a very wealthy man and it is generally seen as habitual for the rich to give to those who are less fortunate than themselves.

Ade Coker and his family stop by to wish Eugene and his family a merry Christmas. Ade Coker is a small, round man who laughs a lot, he plays with his children and he seems like a loving parent. Indeed this description jars with Ade Coker the editor who defies soldiers by writing the truth as editor of the *Standard*. However Ade Coker looks to the future in hope for a better, safer Nigeria.

Ade's family contrasts to Eugene's since Kambili and Jaja are so quiet and demure in comparison to his children. Indeed Ade seems to disapprove of their silence and he jokingly states that it would be very dangerous if no one had the courage to speak up, thus referring to the situation in society at large.

However Kambili and Jaja are more at ease during their stay at Abba since they do not have to follow their rigid timetables. Also life seems to go at a slower pace in Abba and Kambili and Jaja can relax during their Christmas break.

Eugene still maintains his habit of grouping the family to say extremely long prayers which are characterised by silence and a lack of spontaneity. On this particular day, Kambili and Jaja visit their paternal grandfather, Papa-Nnukwu who has refused to convert to Catholicism and he has continued to embrace the traditional Igbo religion. Eugene believes that people who worship pagan gods will face eternal damnation and it is for this reason that he will only allow his children to visit their grandfather for fifteen minutes. Eugene had tried to bribe his father into converting to Catholicism by offering to buy him a house, a car and hiring a driver for him. However Papa–Nnukwu considers it below his standing as an elder in society to convert for such reasons. Indeed Eugene's offer is a contradiction in terms of the Catholic Church's teachings since Eugene tries to tempt Papa-Nnukwu to turn away from his religion by offering materialistic compensation.

Papa-Nnukwu gives much importance to family since he has appealed to the extended family to reach out to Eugene in order to be able to meet his grandchildren. One can see that religion is the reason why Eugene refuses to speak to his father and it is due to his behaviour that his children have never had the opportunity of meeting their grandfather.

Papa-Nnukwu gives Kambili and Jaja a warm welcome and one is immediately struck by how run down his home looks and how he can barely make ends meet, especially when comparing Papa-Nnukwu's modest residence to Eugene's rich home.

Papa-Nnukwu still comes across as a very generous and good-humoured man who truly cares about his grandchildren. Notwithstanding this pleasant disposition, Eugene looks up to Beatrice's father much more than he does his own. Eugene and his family call him grandfather and he is a true convert to Catholicism as well as to Western ways.

Eugene views these two religions as complete opposites, however, Kambili notices the various similarities between Papa-Nnukwu's shrine and their shrine dedicated to Our Lady of Lourdes at home, thus the reader is left to ponder on how different these religions actually are.

Upon getting home, Eugene's rather warped idea of religion becomes apparent as he sends the children to pray for forgiveness since they have stayed with their sickly grandfather longer than they were meant to.

Synopsis – section 2 – chapter 5 (pages 71 to 88)

Aunty Ifeoma comes to visit on the following day and she is immediately characterised by her laughter which pervades the house. Ifeoma gives Kambili a warm hug and she is determined to wake Jaja up when she hears that he has a headache three days before Christmas. She has left her children with Papa-Nnukwu who is telling them a story.

Ifeoma speaks to Beatrice about the many people who usually come to Eugene's house to be fed on Christmas day and that the women help with the cooking so that they can secretly take some meat home with them. Ifeoma wants her children to get to know Eugene's children better and thus suggests taking the children out to a heathen festival. She intends to tell Eugene that they are going out for a drive so that Eugene will agree to let his children spend time with their cousins.

Beatrice takes this opportunity to encourage Ifeoma to take the children to Ifediora, their late father's, home town. However, people from his *umunna* have accused Ifeoma of stealing his money and of killing her husband even though Ifediora died when a trailer rammed into his car. Ifeoma is not offended by these comments and she calmly explained to these people how much she loved and cared for her husband.

Beatrice looks up to Ifeoma and is grateful since Ifeoma had stood by her when others encouraged Eugene to take another wife when Beatrice could not bear more children. Kambili continues to listen to their conversation since Ifeoma's confidence fascinates her. Ifeoma speaks of how no petrol is being delivered to the petrol stations, how she and her fellow lecturers are not being paid and how they have cancelled further strikes. Ifeoma speaks of her friend Phillipa who has moved to America since lecturers are no longer receiving their wages and Ifeoma is reverting to more cost effective ways of cooking at home in order to save money.

Eugene walks past and Ifeoma insists that Eugene should let the children go sightseeing with her and to get to know their cousins better. After much irritation on Eugene's part, Ifeoma accepts to drive past the heathen celebration and Eugene invites them over for Christmas dinner. Ifeoma accepts and her children; Obiora, Amaka and Chima join them.

Amaka immediately asks if they have satellite television but watching television was not included in Kambili and Jaja's timetables and thus Amaka misunderstands why they do not watch television. Ifeoma soon comes to pick up the children, and they intend to pick up Papa-Nnukwu on the way to the *mmuo* festival.

As soon as they arrive at Papa-Nnukwu's house Ifeoma's children rush inside to greet him but Kambili and Jaja stay put as they are not allowed inside the house of a pagan. Papa-Nnukwu is pleasantly surprised to see Kambili and Jaja. However on their way they drive past Eugene's house and Papa-Nnukwu regrets having let Eugene follow the missionaries since he struggles to find food when his son is rich and will not even talk to him. Papa-Nnukwu speaks of when the first missionary, 'Fada' John, came to the village and would speak to the children about Catholicism in the afternoons.

They approach the crowded *mmuo* festival and they see a pretty female *mmuo* pass by and Kambili remembers Eugene describing this festival as a dangerous pagan festival. The next *mmuo* is a powerful and gruesomely dressed figure and Papa-Nnukwu tells the girls not to look at it. At this point Jaja comments on there being people under the masks at the festival and Papa-Nnukwu tells him off for this. Aunty Ifeoma asks if Jaja has done the *ima mmuo*, the initiation into the spirit world and to manhood, but Jaja has not. Ifeoma takes the children home and Kambili dreams of laughing.

Analysis – section 2 – chapter 5 (pages 71 to 88)

Upon meeting Aunty Ifeoma, Kambili is immediately enchanted by her as she is not used to seeing such a determined woman with such a charismatic character. Aunty Ifeoma is a joy to be around especially since she laughs continuously. Ifeoma is described as a woman who resembles Eugene as she is tall and trim like Eugene.

The reader also gets to know Papa-Nnukwu better as he accompanies the rest of them to the *mmuo* festival. One realises that Papa-Nnukwu has a particular habit of telling his grandchildren stories and these stories serve to expand Ifeoma's children's knowledge of African culture and since Kambili and Jaja are not in close contact with Papa-Nnukwu their knowledge of African culture is rather limited.

Aunty Ifeoma represents the African woman who is very proud of her Igbo culture and she freely uses Igbo terms in normal conversations such as when she converses with Beatrice.

Beatrice and Ifeoma go on to speak about women's roles in society. Beatrice insists that a woman cannot live without a man in her life but Ifeoma says that women only *think* that they need a man. Ifeoma is a lecturer at the University of Nsukka and she speaks about her female students who study, get a degree and then get married. Marriage for these women means that they must tend to their husband first and they no longer have the opportunity to put what they have studied into practice. Beatrice, on the other hand, insists that a woman is nothing without a husband and that every woman wants to get married.

Ifeoma also speaks of how the new military government is slowly bringing the country to its knees by not paying lecturers, not supplying basic needs such as petrol and gas at affordable prices. People are thus finding it impossible to earn a living and are consequently turning to other countries such as America for a better future.

Ifeoma's three children soon join them. Obiora is Ifeoma's eldest boy and he has thick glasses and he smiles continuously, whilst Amaka is Ifeoma's only girl and she is fifteen like Kambili. However, Amaka is a much more confident and forthcoming whilst Kamibli is quiet and reserved. Chima, on the other hand, is Ifeoma's youngest boy and he is but seven years old. One notes that all of Ifeoma's children have questioning and intelligent eyes but Kambili perceives Ifeoma's eyes as warm.

The issue regarding religion immediately comes into focus when Ifeoma takes the children out and they pick up Papa-Nnukwu on their way to the festival. Ifeoma and her children are open to different religions. Indeed Ifeoma calls Papa-Nnukwu a "traditionalist" but Kambili and Jaja refrain from entering his house as he is a pagan.

The atmosphere in the car is full of laughter and conversation as Papa-Nnukwu joins the group. However as Ifeoma drives past Eugene's house, Papa-Nnukwu's sadness soon becomes apparent as he thinks of his son who has turned away from him. Ifeoma is quick to point out that Eugene turned away from his father because of his character and not because of religion since Ifeoma is a Catholic and she takes care of her father whilst Eugene has shunned him.

At the *mmuo* festival one notices how women are meant to be pretty and harmless. On the other hand men, as represented by the *mmuo* as powerful, influential and they are the ones who inspire fear in those around them. During the festival the fact that Kambili and Jaja are ignorant of many Igbo traditions becomes obvious and Jaja feels that there is something missing since he has not taken part in certain celebrations and rituals.

Synopsis – section 2 – chapter 6 (pages 89 to 109)

The Achike family goes to mass on Christmas day at St Paul's and they meet Aunty Ifeoma and her children coming out of mass. Ifeoma is wearing a red wrapper and Amaka is wearing the same red lipstick as her mother. During mass Kambili soon realises that the sermon is focused on collecting funds for the church rather than on conveying any spiritual message. They are seated in the front row with other important people and they attend a fund raiser for the parish priest's home after mass where Eugene donates a generous sum even though he is extremely annoyed by the focus on money. People touch Eugene's white tunic as he exits and they go home to find many people who are waiting for Eugene and some women are cooking in the backyard.

Ifeoma and her children reach Eugene's house for Christmas lunch and they admire his house. Amaka speaks of playing the stereo which Kambili and Jaja never use, as time for such activities does not feature in their schedules. Ifeoma and her children are full of praise as they admire the stereo, the bathrooms and so on. They go downstairs to greet the Igwe, who is very important to the Igbo community and Beatrice greets him in the traditional way whilst Ifeoma and her children bow in respect of the Igwe and this irritates Eugene.

While Obiora is playing cards with Chima, and Amaka and Jaja are talking about a book Kambili happens to overhear a conversation between Ifeoma and Beatrice. Beatrice tries to convince Ifeoma to let Eugene give her some gas cylinders but Ifeoma does not want to since Eugene will consequently expect changes in her behaviour and so Ifeoma does not want to be indebted to him. When Ifediora, Ifeoma's late husband, was alive he used to tell Eugene what he thinks of him to his face.

Soon after they sit down to dinner and Eugene spends twenty minutes saying prayers and Ifeoma chides him for this but Eugene pretends to be unflustered. As they eat, Ifeoma tries to convince Eugene to send the children to Nsukka for a week, but Eugene offers no reply and so she continues to insist, she even challenges Eugene to tell her when he called her last. Eugene does not pursue the discussion, instead he toasts to the glory of God but Ifeoma promptly toasts to the spirit of the family. Amaka states that the fruit juice produced at Eugene's factory is too sweet. Amaka goes on to speak of the apparitions of the Blessed Virgin in Aokpe and Ifeoma suggests sending Kambili and Jaja to Nsukka so that she can take them on a pilgrimage to Aokpe.

On the following morning, Kambili gets her period and cramps wreak havoc on her stomach. Beatrice tells Kambili to take some cereal before swallowing some panadols even though there is less than an hour left before mass. Eugene walks in to find Kambili eating the cereal Beatrice and Jaja watching and he is so furious that he punishes all three of them with his heavy leather belt. Jaja tries to take the blame in order to protect his mother and sister but to no avail.

After punishing them Eugene asks if they are hurt and he hugs them close to him. They go to a later mass and they leave Abba after New Year's Day. They encounter a road block as they drive along and they see that there has been a road accident. Kambili also notes that the road block has been set up at a dangerous place for the motorists but it is conveniently situated next to the bushes where they can hide the bribes they collect for letting people through.

Eugene phones Ifeoma on the feast of the Epiphany and the Achike family go to Father Benedict to confess on this day. Eugene had refused to confess to the priest at Abba because he thought the priest was not as spiritual as Father

Benedict. Kambili and her family go to confession and when it is Kambili's turn Father Benedict prompts her to list *all* her sins. He is satisfied once she says that she stayed longer at her grandfather's house than she was meant to and that she watched the pagan masquerades at the *mmuo* festival. Eugene is very happy on their way back home and Beatrice reminds Eugene to send some gas cylinders along with the children as they will be setting off for Ifeoma's house on the following day. The children are enthusiastic as well as nervous about going to Ifeoma's and Kevin drives the two of them to Nsukka where they will stay for a week.

Analysis – section 2 – chapter 6 (page 89 to 109)

As the Achike family goes to mass on Christmas day, the thematic focus of the novel turns yet again to religion. Eugene disapproves of how Catholicism is presented to the congregation at Abba since the parish priest mainly focuses on how much money they are able to collect rather than conveying a spiritual message. One also notes preferential treatment is bestowed on the wealthier members of the congregation as their seats are reserved in the front row and people regard these members of the congregation with respect.

Upon getting home they immediately realise that women have already started cooking in the backyard and this is the villagers' way of showing respect towards this very rich and important person in their village. The villagers have also gone a step further and they have bestowed a title on Eugene in the past, this title is *Omelora* and it means The One Who Does for the Community.

The women who have come to cook also devote much of their attention to Jaja who would be a good match for their daughters since he would inherit his father's wealth in the future.

As soon as Ifeoma's children step into Eugene's house their attention immediately gravitates towards the different forms of entertainment which may be found in the Achike household such as music and watching television. However this immediately puts Kambili and Jaja at a loss since they do not have time to enjoy music or to form an opinion about what type of music they prefer. This hesitation is however misunderstood by Amaka since she thinks that Kambili and Jaja are snobs and that they feel superior to Amaka and her brothers.

As the two families are conversing and looking around, the Igwe pays them an unexpected visit and Eugene's religious attitudes take precedence once more. The Igwe had converted but he still let others carry out pagan sacrifices in his home and it is for this reason that Eugene had shunned the Igwe and he had discontinued his visits to the Igwe's house. One can thus see how Eugene's scrupulous observation of religious rules leads him to turn away from people.

At a certain point Kambili manages to overhear a conversation between Ifeoma and Beatrice and it is here that Ifeoma may be seen as the stronger of the two women. Ifeoma finds it hard to make ends meet since her husband passed away and she has to raise three children on her own. To make matters worse lecturers are not being paid for their work. However, in spite of all of this, Ifeoma still refuses to accept financial help from Eugene, thus adhering to what she believes is best.

Indeed Ifeoma openly expresses her criticism of Eugene to Beatrice when she says that Eugene takes too much upon himself when he turns away his own ailing father because of religious reasons. Also when they sit down to dinner Ifeoma tries to convince Eugene to do what she says and he does not even try to contradict her when she tries to convince him to let her take the children out because he knows how headstrong she is.

Family is the most important thing to Ifeoma and she gets what she wants in the end. She knows that Eugene gives much importance to religion and so she uses the idea of a pilgrimage to Aokpe, mentioned by Amaka, for the children to be able to come to Nsukka and get to know each other better.

On the following day, Kambili suffers from period pains and chooses to take some cereal and panadols after Beatrice has encouraged her to do so. It is through this incident that one is made aware of Eugene's scrupulous observance of religious rules, in this case of fasting before receiving the Eucharist. Eugene refuses to hear about Kambili being physically unwell and he flies into a rage at seeing her breaking the Eucharistic fast and the others idly watching her. He therefore physically punishes all three of them and as is characteristic of Eugene, he asks them how they are after such behaviour and he seems anxious to see to them after the incident. Eugene however insists on punishing them as he believes that it is for the best.

When they are on the road later in the day, they come across a road block. It is here that the military leaders' greed comes to the forefront. This is due to the fact that they position the road block in a way which is convenient to them but which puts the motorists at risk and is consequently extremely dangerous.

The Achike family finally makes their way to confession and their confessor is Father Benedict. It is here that Father Benedict is seen as an extremely intrusive person as he oversteps his role as confessor and tells Kambili that he knows that she has other sins to confess. After confession the children soon prepare their things and set off for Ifeoma's house at Nsukka. However, before they leave Eugene gives them a schedule to follow during their week at Ifeoma's, thus he still tries to control them even when they are at a distance.

Synopsis – section 2 – chapter 7 (pages 110 to 139)

Kambili and Jaja approach Nsukka which is more run down in terms of appearance. In fact burnt cars are simply left by the roadside, dust covers signs, cars and so on. They pass through a road block and Kevin throws money to the guards. They drive past the University of Nsukka and Kambili's attention is caught by a statue of a large black lion and the university's motto which is 'To restore the dignity of man'.

Aunty Ifeoma gives them a warm welcome and she shows them around her flat. Kambili is immediately struck by the low roof of Ifeoma's flat, but Ifeoma shows them around the flat as soon as they enter and she tries to make them feel at home. She invites them into the kitchen and they talk as she cooks.

Ifeoma's children soon get home and the children welcome their new guests. Jaja goes out with Obiora and Chima to buy some drinks and Kambili is left with Amaka who invites Kambili into her room and she speaks of music and painting.

They all sit down to a meal of chicken and soft drinks which is unusual in this household. Ifeoma's children enjoy the meal immensely and they converse freely; Kambili is surprised at how much they talk. Ifeoma encourages Kambili to eat and Amaka misunderstands Kambili's silence and shyness at table for snobbery.

After dinner Eugene phones to remind his children to study and pray. Later on that evening, they have dinner and Ifeoma's children sit in the living room as they watch television. It is at this point that Jaja finds the courage to take out the schedule that Eugene had given him. Ifeoma takes the schedule from them and insists that they do as she says since they are in her house. Ifeoma and the children say the rosary as they usually do and that night Kambili dreams that Amaka is drowning her.

Kambili wakes up the following day and the children go to get water. They start the day by saying a prayer and having breakfast and then they all head out to visit the university and Father Amadi joins them for dinner that evening. However on the way out, Jaja stops to admire Ifeoma's purple hibiscus and the other plants which decorate the garden.

They drive past the university primary school which Chima attends and the Institute of African Studies which is where Ifeoma lectures. They drive through the hostel's quarter, where Amaka wants to stay once she joins the university, the servants' quarters and the residential area. Kambili thinks of how Eugene will probably decide which university she will frequent in the future. Ifeoma drives past the VC and the professors' residences and she refers to riots that had taken place in this area. They drive past the statue of the preening lion and Jaja and Obiora question the meaning of the motto, 'To restore man's dignity'.

They head for home and Amaka, Ifeoma and Kambili start cooking as Father Amadi is coming over for dinner, but Amaka teases Kambili since she does not know how to cook. Father Amadi tries to involve Kambili and Jaja in the conversation during dinner and he speaks of having said mass at the church of St Agnes. He also speaks admiringly of Eugene and about how Amnesty World is about to give him an award and this makes Kambili very proud. They speak of Aokpe and Amaka and Father Amadi discuss the veracity of the apparitions and then they say the rosary and sing Igbo songs. Father Amadi comments on how Kambili has not laughed or smiled since he arrived and Kambili goes to her room.

Analysis – section 2 – chapter 7 (pages 110 to 139)

A gradual change in setting informs the reader that Kambili and Jaja are approaching Nsukka. The cars they drive by are full of dust as are the traffic signs; the roads are full of potholes, thus implying that Nsukka is a poorer town than Enugu. Kevin drives past the more expensive properties, such as the duplexes and bungalows, which are situated next the university. However these properties become more and more inexpensive until they reach a part of Nsukka where blocks of flats are built and this is where Ifeoma and her family lives. The block of flats Ifeoma lives in looks quite rundown but a garden patch in front of Ifeoma's flat is full of a variety of plants with vibrant colours and this helps to liven up the appearance of this part of town.

Once inside Ifeoma's flat it becomes immediately obvious to Kambili and Jaja that Ifeoma finds it hard to make ends meet because of various features which need attention and due to the discordant decorations. Notwithstanding this Ifeoma does her best to make Kambili and Jaja feel welcome in her home and to make them feel like members of the family.

Jaja is very enthusiastic about their visit to Ifeoma's house and he is keen to enjoy his stay, however, Kambili who is extremely shy, finds it more difficult to relax and integrate with her relatives.

As soon as Ifeoma's children come home, Amaka immediately comes across a dominant character. Amaka always speaks with confidence and she is therefore quite surprised to find that Kambili speaks in whispers as this seems quite out of place at Nsukka. She is also very fond of Igbo culture and music and one can thus see that she resembles Ifeoma a great deal.

Once at table Kambili is surprised to see how communication is free and uninhibited. It seems as if every opinion is appreciated and everyone is sure to make their voice heard and this seems to make Ifeoma very proud.

Amaka however soon picks up on Kambili's persistent silence at table and this is misinterpreted by Amaka as snobbery and a feeling of superiority towards Ifeoma and her children. Amaka thinks Kambili looks down on them because they are poorer than Eugene's family but Kambili is simply shy and timid due to her father's controlling influence. It is for this reason that Kambili suffers Amaka's insolence in silence. Amaka is told off by Ifeoma and Obiora but Kambili does not retaliate.

After dinner, Jaja finds the courage to mention their schedule to Ifeoma. Eugene's insistence on trying to control the children whilst they are at a distance angers Ifeoma and she immediately confiscates the schedule and insists that Eugene will not be the one to decide what they do while they are at Nsukka.

Ifeoma also gives due importance to religion as is seen when they say the rosary in the evening and they say a morning prayer on the following day. However Ifeoma's prayers are different since they sing Igbo songs as they say the rosary during their morning prayer, Ifeoma prays for laughter which implies that those involved are fully enjoying each other's company.

As they are setting off for a visit to the university, Jaja stops to admire the plants in Ifeoma's garden, in particular her purple hibiscus. Ifeoma takes prestigious care of her precious plants and Jaja is immediately drawn to the purple hibiscus which is a symbol of the freedom that Kambili and Jaja taste during their stay at Ifeoma's house.

As they drive through the residential area surrounding the university, Ifeoma mentions the riots that have happened in the past. Ifeoma mentions past riots since she wants her children to be in touch with social attitudes and what is going on around them, also because rioting was quite a common occurrence.

That evening Kambili and Jaja are introduced to Father Amadi who is a close friend of Ifeoma's family. Kambili is initially struck by the young, casual appearance of this priest. Father Amadi also has the talent of putting people at ease as he tries to rope everyone into the conversation. When Father Amadi mentions knowing Eugene and having said mass at the parish of St Agnes, Ifeoma seems rather reluctant to mention that Eugene is her brother since she knows how reserved Eugene is and how critical he must have been of Father Amadi. Kambili is also surprised by the fact that Amaka and Obiora discuss ideas in such a detailed and mature way, that it is obvious to an onlooker that they are used to expressing their own opinions and justifying their arguments to others.

Synopsis – section 2 – chapter 8 (pages 140 – 161)

Life at Ifeoma's house always included laughter, prayers and Igbo songs. Ifeoma's house is always clean and this is because the housework is equally distributed amongst the children. However, Amaka insists on doing the housework that Kambili has done again as she claims that Kambili does not clean well.

One day Amaka's friends come over and they spend their time chatting about school, American magazines and so on. At a certain point one of Amaka's friends asks Kambili a very casual question but Kambili gets tongue-tied and she rushes out of the room which surprises Amaka and her friends.

Amaka decides to ask Ifeoma if there is something wrong with Jaja and Kambili since they act strangely but Ifeoma insists that she should respect her cousins. Meanwhile Jaja is watching television with Obiora and Kambili goes out to help Ifeoma with the gardening, however children from the other apartments come to speak to them and Kambili is at a loss when approached by them. Ifeoma realises this and thus suggests that Kambili should read a book. Kambili therefore sits reading on the veranda as Jaja is weeding.

Ifeoma speaks of how Jaja got his nickname; when Jaja was young, "Jaja" was all that he could say and they thus continued to call him Jaja instead of Chukwuka. Ifeoma approved of Jaja keeping the name since it is reminiscent of Jaja of Opobo, who did not let the British take over all of the trade and he was exiled to the West Indies for taking such a stand. They talk about this defiant king and Jaja contributes to the discussion on whether it is worth being defiant in life or not.

At a certain point Chima comments on Jaja's gnarled finger and Ifeoma changes the subject immediately. Kambili remembers how Eugene had done this to Jaja when he was ten years old since he had not come first in his Holy Communion class. Eugene was in tears once he had realised what he had done to Jaja's finger and he had taken Jaja to hospital later on.

They receive an unexpected call from Beatrice since soldiers have found the secret offices of the *Standard* and they destroyed the machinery, closed off the premises and arrested Ade Coker. This means that the children's stay at Nsukka will be extended since soldiers went to Eugene's house and shot Eugene to make sure that he never published again. Kambili and Jaja regret what has happened back at Enugu but they are also overjoyed that they will be extending their stay.

Father Amadi is to pick Jaja and Obiora up to play football and Kambili is also invited. However Ifeoma is worried about Papa-Nnukwu since he is sick and she would like to bring him to Nsukka to live with them. Father Amadi offers to give Ifeoma some fuel so that she can pick Papa-Nnukwu up.

Father Amadi comes over on the following day and he lets Obiora suck fuel from his car and Ifeoma is grateful for his help. Obiora then accompanies Ifeoma as she goes to pick up Papa-Nnukwu. Meanwhile Amaka plays her music loudly and Jaja is busy cutting the grass. Kambili approaches Jaja as he is at work and asks if they are normal but Jaja does not reply.

Ifeoma brings a tired Papa-Nnukwu into the house and he greets all of them. However, he chooses to lie down on the floor even though Amaka offers him her bed. The doctors are on strike and so Ifeoma has arranged with Doctor Nduoma to come to see Papa-Nnukwu since he lives in the same street. Dr Nduoma comes to see Papa-Nnukwu and Jaja shows some concern about Eugene finding out about Papa-Nnukwu but he is not as worried as he would usually be.

Jaja tells Kambili that he spoke to Ifeoma about what happened to his finger and Kambili is taken aback since they had never spoken of Eugene's violence to others. Jaja goes off to wipe down Ifeoma's car, even though he had never washed a car before at home. Dr Nduoma leaves and Ifeoma thanks Jaja for his help. Papa-Nnukwu needs to have some tests done and so Ifeoma takes him to the medical centre on the following day, only to find that the workers are on strike and that they will have to go to a private lab, which would be more costly.

So instead Ifeoma buys the medicine prescribed by the doctor. In the evening, Papa-Nnukwu starts to feel better and while he is eating, Amaka shows her concern for him. However, the tension seems to have subsided as they all come together and while Papa-Nnukwu is distracted by his grandchildren's banter, Ifeoma inserts his medicine into his food just in case he refuses to take it, as he grumbles that the tablets are bitter. Obiora compares the sense of taste to morality by pondering that they are both relative. Nobody seems to catch on to his observations; instead Papa-Nnukwu continues muttering that he is being treated like a child just because he is old. Amaka is feeling downhearted as they cannot watch television as the lights go out due to the imposed curfew. Obiora suggests that their grandfather could talk about his folk stories as they used to do when they lived in Abba. Kambili notices how strong the bond is between Papa-Nnukwu and Ifeoma's children, as they laugh wholeheartedly at his comments. Chima asks him to recount one of his favourite stories.

Clearing his throat, Papa-Nnukwu narrates the tale of how the tortoise got its cracked shell: a group of animals were facing a long period of famine when one day Tortoise discovered that Dog, his mother and her friends were enjoying themselves up in the trees and were not suffering at all from hunger. Threatening to tell the other animals, Tortoise blackmails Dog into taking him up to where his family is staying so that he could eat abundantly. But one day, Tortoise oversteps Dog's pact and decides to imitate Dog's voice to be let up the tree. When Dog realises what Tortoise is up to, he shouts to his mother to cut the rope and Tortoise comes tumbling down, thus cracking his shell.

Analysis – section 2 – chapter 8 (pages 140 – 161)

When Amaka's friends come over to spend time with Amaka, they are rather taken aback to find that Kambili cannot sustain a conversation with them and that she simply flees when she is spoken to. This is yet again due to Kambili's shyness which is a result of a controlling father. On the other hand, Jaja feels quite at ease at Ifeoma's place and he seems to be thoroughly enjoying his stay as he helps out in the garden and with other household chores that he would usually shy away from at home.

The reader is also further exposed to Ifeoma's generous and understanding nature in this section as she quickly removes Kambili from an awkward situation and suggests that she read a book which might be more to her liking.

Another aspect of Ifeoma's character is also emphasised when they discuss how Jaja got his nickname, as his real name is Chukwuka. Ifeoma is full of praise for Jaja of Opobo, who was a king who fought to defend his country and Ifeoma respects such strength of character and patriotism.

The conversation focuses on Jaja and it is Jaja's gnarled finger that catches Chima's attention. The reader is thus, yet again, presented with proof of how violent Eugene can be and in this case Eugene has left an indelible mark. Also as is habitual with Eugene, he feels sorry for what he has done only after the punishment has been inflicted and the damage done.

The unexpected phone call from Beatrice draws the reader's attention to the chaotic social situation once again. Social unrest is increasing and the soldiers are resorting to violence to make sure that the people do what they would like. Soldiers seem to be co-ordinating themselves better as they work in large numbers when they target someone, in this case the offices of the *Standard* which the soldiers destroy. The other newspapers barely mention what has happened to the *Standard* as they do not want to antagonise those in power.

Notwithstanding this, Ifeoma's major concern at this point in time is her ailing father. Ifeoma is determined to invite Papa-Nnukwu to stay with her and the children so that she can take better care of him. Father Amadi is also seen to be quite similar to Ifeoma in terms of his generosity and altruism. Indeed, Father Amadi jumps at the chance to help Papa-Nnukwu even though he is not a Catholic. Father Amadi is also ready to help Papa-Nnukwu even though he is a heathen and he willingly extends a helping hand to aid this person.

Change is also apparent in Kambili as she begins to question their way of life and whether it is normal. This is a direct result of being exposed to a different way of life at Ifeoma's house and because she has distanced herself from Eugene. Jaja also grows increasingly fond of Ifeoma and trusts her with information regarding Eugene's violent punishments. Jaja appreciates her attention and concern and it is for this reason that he wipes down her car; something he would never do at home. Jaja seems to relax after having told their secret to an outsider and this is seen in his peaceful afternoon activities.

Obiora is growing quickly into the responsible man of the house. He has to take up certain duties in order to help his mother pull through difficult times. This underlines how childhood in a country which is as corrupt and violent as Nigeria, is continuously threatened and short-lived. Amaka too is conditioned by the political turmoil as she listens to culturally conscious musicians. Such political turmoil is reflected in the strikes called upon by doctors and their medical centres, by the exorbitant prices that smaller clinics demand thereby taking advantage of people's illnesses in times of adversity, by the continuous lack of fuel and even in the story that Papa-Nnukwu narrates.

Whilst Papa-Nnukwu tells this tale and his grandchildren end up laughing, they learn an important lesson, that beneath an innocent story, famine brings out the worst in men and animals alike and that greed and selfishness consequently abound, leading to more poverty and inequality.

Synopsis – section 2 – chapter 9 (pages 162 to 205)

The next day, Ifeoma and Amaka discuss Papa-Nnukwu's stay over breakfast. Amaka suggests that her grandfather should live with them instead of going back to his mud hut where he is not taken care of properly, not even by the village girl (Chinyelu) who assists him. Ifeoma, however, knows that very soon her father will start arguing about wanting to go back to his village so in the meantime Ifeoma will try to get the tests done. The only problem is that she has to go to the bank first to withdraw the money she will need to pay the expensive medical bill, and that means queuing up for long hours at both the bank and the labs, so that by the time she gets to the latter, they will have closed. As they are trying to think of a solution, Father Amadi turns up and offers to take Jaja and Obiora to the stadium in the evening, to play football with some of the boys from the seminary. In the meantime, Kambili had already ran inside to avoid meeting Father Amadi, even though she is pleased when she hears him ask for her and he even invites her to join them. Although she declines the invitation, she wishes she could run after his car when she hears them leave.

Kambili thus spends the evening with Papa-Nnukwu and Amaka, when her grandfather tells her how much he admires his granddaughter for her artistic talents but is somewhat sad to see that she is not painting the shrines of his gods anymore like she used to in the old days.

Kambili wonders whether his moaning about the old days is a direct consequence of the strong medications and at the same time observes Amaka who is arranging her grandfather's hair so that she can paint his portrait. As she stood watching them together, Kambili could not help but be in awe of their special relationship, something she would be deprived of forever. She is mesmerised by the almost magical atmosphere they seem to create between them so much so that she cannot even move; finally, she leaves Amaka to her painting and goes to the kitchen where she finds Ifeoma who notices that Kambili is almost in tears. As Kambili puts it down to something that has got into her eyes, Ifeoma asks her niece to help her with the cooking, even though Ifeoma does not seem convinced by Kambili's answer.

Ifeoma turns the conversation around to speak of her father, and she is very relieved to see that he has enough strength to pose for Amaka. As soon as she mentions that it is thanks to Our Lady, Kambili questions whether it is possible for Our Lady to intercede on behalf of a heathen. Ifeoma is unable to answer Kambili initially but then explains that Papa-Nnukwu is a traditionalist and not a heathen and that he prays just like them. Kambili, however, drifts off to hear Amaka and Papa-Nnukwu's laughter in the living room and starts to imagine that if she were to go in there, they would stop laughing.

When Ifeoma next awakens Kambili, she asks her to watch over Papa-Nnukwu who was on the veranda. Kambili feels anxious about this as she has been trying to avoid direct contact with what her father deemed to be a pagan, even though the former was Papa-Nnukwu's son. Kambili feels more uncomfortable when she witnesses her grandfather reciting his invocations to his gods, asking them to bless him and others, and to lift the "curse" on his son who has forsaken him. As she stands observing him in detail, she finally notices that after his prayers he smiled and then remembers that Jaja and herself never smile after they say the rosary with their parents.

Back on the veranda, Amaka joins her grandfather and scrubs his feet before resuming her portrait. She decides that the veranda is a better place to paint because she can catch the sunlight falling on his skin. Ifeoma asks Kambili to help her do the *orah* leaves before cooking but an embarrassed Kambili confesses that she does not know how to prepare *orah*, at which Ifeoma calls Amaka to do it instead. Amaka, however, intent on continuing her portrait is irritated by Kambili's inaptitude and retorts that just because Kambili is rich does not mean she can be excused from cooking; after all, Amaka continues, Kambili will eat from the same food so she could help prepare it. Ifeoma is angry at Kambili for not rebutting Amaka's insult, at which Kambili calmly asks her cousin to lower her voice and explains that although she does not know how to cook something she is willing to learn if someone is equally willing to teach her. Amaka relents and together they prepare the *orah* leaves for the soup. Meanwhile, Ifeoma has gone shopping and when she returns she is irritated that food costs more now. Since fuel is a rarity, transportation costs have increased and consequently food is more expensive.

As they are discussing the rise in the cost of living, Father Amadi comes around and they start talking about a friend of his who had just come from Papua New Guinea after having narrowly escaped a crocodile attack. Ifeoma is concerned about Father Amadi going to dangerous places and Amaka is sad at the thought of Father Amadi leaving them. Papa-Nnukwu feels lost in their conversation and so Amaka explains that Father Amadi appertains to a group of missionary priests who visit different countries in order to convert people to Catholicism. Papa-Nnukwu is almost shocked to hear that the black man is now being asked to do the white man's job in the white man's land and remembering his own brush with the Catholic religion, he pleads with Father Amadi to be always truthful and never tell people to disrespect their elders as his son has been doing since he had converted to Catholicism. Father Amadi tries to reassure Papa-Nnukwu by informing him that he goes to places that need a priest and that he will do his best to speak the truth. Obiora underlines their conversations by using a culinary metaphor: when you cook, once you mix the ingredients, you will not be able to separate one ingredient from the other; and for Obiora, it is the same with religion and oppression which once intertwined cannot be distinguished from each other. Father Amadi is not overjoyed with Obiora's critical sense of observation and is concerned that at such a young age Obiora is demonstrating early signs of madness. Amaka, however, supports her brother and reiterates that it is typical for priests and unfair on their behalf to label people as being mad merely because religion and its go-betweens are challenged.

Father Amadi still tries to have his say when he compares Amaka and Obiora to Kambili by praising her for not wasting her time over constant arguing even though he knows that she sits quietly thinking over and weighing other people's words. Turning to Kambili, he comments that she did not want to go with them to the stadium, at which Kambili stutters that she was asleep. So Father Amadi offers to take only her this time and that she could play or just watch. Amaka intrudes upon their conversation and remarks that Kambili is 'frightened to death'. Ifeoma reassures Kambili that it will be fun and suggests that Kambili should change into more comfortable clothes, preferably shorts, to fight off the heat due to the fact that there are no roofs shielding the spectator stands. As usual, Amaka wants to have her say by stating that the money intended for the stadium was misappropriated by corrupt individuals. Kambili does not mind Amaka's comment as she is worried about something more personal: she does not have shorts because she was used to wearing long skirts. However, Kambili is tempted enough to put on some lipstick but as she leaves the house, she feels guilty of being vain and wipes it off with the back of her hand.

On their way to the stadium Father Amadi and Kambili talk about Papa-Nnukwu; in confession-like mode, Kambili feels guilty about sharing the same room with her grandfather because she believes he is a 'heathen' at which Father Amadi responds that that is what she was taught to believe by her father. Father Amadi seems to know what has been going on back home and this is because he has been talking to Jaja, who apparently has let him in on things that they were not meant to talk about.

All sorts of questions about what Jaja could have told Father Amadi start creeping into Kambili's head but after a fleeting moment they are at the stadium and Father Amadi asks her if she would like to play. She admits that she does not know how to play and comes up with the excuse that when she was younger, nobody liked to pick her for volleyball so she did not bother with sports. Father Amadi then asks her about Jesus and before he starts running, he challenges her to catch him so as to show him how much she loves Jesus. She runs after him but does not manage to catch up with him the first time so he gives her another four chances but she still does not succeed; yet, he is pleased with her efforts and, pointing out that she has good legs for running, he suggests that she should try running more often. She realises that his eyes were on her legs and feels it was too intimate a moment and therefore avoids eye contact with him.

After commenting on her lipstick mark, the boys who are coached by Father Amadi arrive and Kambili observes how they were all dressed in ragged and torn clothes and yet they are so jovial and enthusiastic about playing football. So as Kambili watches them play, she wonders whether the boys felt the same way as she did when she was with Father Amadi, considering that when he was with her he gave her his full attention. On their way back home, Father Amadi plays a tape and Kambili recognises the tune as being the same one her mother sang when she and Jaja went home with their report cards.

After singing to the tune, Father Amadi asks Kambili if she enjoyed the game and he goes on to explain that he sees Christ in the boys' faces; he then talks to them and tells her that most of the boys have stopped going to school because their families have fallen on hard times. One of them in particular, Ekwueme, was actually attending Nsukka High School before his father, who was a driver at the university, lost his job; consequently, Ekwueme had to start working as a bus conductor but to Father Amadi's relief, he is doing very well.

Father Amadi comments that Kambili has not asked him any questions all the while he has been talking and Kambili is perplexed as she feels she does not know what to ask. He suggests that she should learn the 'art of questioning' from Amaka and after he makes her laugh, Kambili asks what led him to priesthood. He confesses that he wanted to be a doctor at first but upon hearing a priest speak he had heard the calling.

Kambili is taken by this but after stating that he was just joking about it, Father Amadi admits that it is quite a complex question to address but he explains that priesthood was the vocation that came close to answering many questions he had while growing up. Before dropping Kambili off, Father Amadi tells her that he has enjoyed the afternoon in her company and offers her to go with him to the stadium in the near future. Although Kambili felt shy about giving him a straight answer, she felt good and her chest felt light. This feeling of being lifted off the ground is short-lived, however, as Ifeoma who looked tense, informs her that Eugene had phoned that same afternoon and that he had found out that Papa-Nnukwu was living with them and that consequently, his children were constantly in the presence of a heathen.

Kambili is now worried that her father will be angry at them for not having told him themselves and Ifeoma tries to calm her down by telling her that she has managed to convince

Eugene that she will drive them back home in a couple of days, just enough time to get fuel. As an afterthought, Ifeoma remarks that Eugene had succeeded in releasing Ade Coker from prison, but Kambili felt too overwhelmed by what would happen to take note of such news.

Whilst Kambili imagines her father raging against her in her sleep, Amaka awakens her and walks over to wake Papa-Nnukwu, only to discover that he is not responding. As Ifeoma attempts to stir him, they realise that he has died in his sleep. Everyone is shocked by his sudden passing away, but Kambili still notices that her brother moves forward towards the inert body of their grandfather, and she is afraid that her father will be outraged if he finds out that Jaja was sitting so close to Papa-Nnukwu and even touched him. Amaka rushes off crying and Kambili observes that her cousin did not need to cry silently as she herself had learnt to do.

Papa-Nnukwu is carried away by two men brought by Doctor Nduoma and before leaving for the mortuary, Ifeoma points out to Kambili that at least Papa-Nnukwu had died smiling. Amaka regrets not having finished her grandfather's portrait and blames the medical centre and the strike for her Papa-Nnukwu's death. Ifeoma reassures her that Papa-Nnukwu's death was only natural, given his old age and recurrent illness.

In all the commotion, Eugene arrives unannounced and Kambili's attention is diverted to him and to what punishment awaits her for having clearly disobeyed him. Even though Ifeoma is irritated by her brother's unwanted visit, she informs him of their father's death and he insists that he pays for the funeral on the condition that their father is converted to Catholicism during the ceremony. Ifeoma quarrels with her brother and would rather sell her husband's grave than do what Eugene demands. Before Ifeoma can press her point any further, he leads Kambili and Jaja out and they leave, Amaka rushes out and hands something wrapped in black cellophane to Kambili: Papa-Nnukwu's unfinished portrait.

Back home, Beatrice is equally shocked to learn of Papa-Nnukwu's death but Eugene is harsh and states that his father will now face judgement. Jaja responds by saying that perhaps his grandfather did not want to convert. Eugene is taken aback and blames his son's sudden change in behaviour on living with a 'heathen'. Jaja further challenges his father by asking if he could be given a key to his bedroom and Eugene angrily questions him about what use is a key if not to commit sins against his body. They eat dinner in silence that evening and when Beatrice asks Kambili how she feels about returning, the latter wishes she could tell her mother how different it feels to be back home, how she had got used to the warmth of Ifeoma's home and could not feel the same about the empty space, the high ceilings and the lifeless surroundings of her own home. Eugene interrupts their conversation as he summons Kambili upstairs.

Afraid of an imminent punishment, Kambili goes up nonetheless and finds her father in the bathroom. He orders her to get in the bath and starts preaching about the sin she has committed: that of being near a heathen and not telling him about it. He starts pouring scalding water over her legs, whilst crying and telling her that she should strive for perfection. Kambili tries to contain her emotions but screams when the pain becomes unbearable. Beatrice rushes in to whisk Kambili away from further torture. Whilst Kambili feels her feet swelling and voices concerning going to school in such a condition, she imagines that it would be the same for Jaja. Later that night, Eugene enters Kambili's bedroom to explain what had happened to him when he tried to commit a sin against his body and was punished by one of the fathers at St Gregory's, who soaked Eugene's hand in boiling water; Eugene wants Kambili and Jaja to know that what he does is for their own good. However, after her father leaves, Kambili thinks of Papa-Nnukwu's painting in her bag rather than of what her father had done and said to her.

The next day she decides to show Jaja the painting and after he had ran his fingers over it, he decided that he also had something to show her: stalks of purple hibiscus. They both rush to hide their secret presents as they hear their father approaching. During lunch, Eugene surprises everyone by telling them that he did send Ifeoma money for the funeral after all, even though he had misgivings about them being used to sacrifice animals and organise a pagan feast. Nevertheless, Beatrice is pleased that he relented to Ifeoma's pleas.

That evening, Eugene is preoccupied with more important matters as he greets several guests, among them his editor Ade Coker. The latter is frustrated over a story that he would like to run, but has been warned against doing so, for the man who Ade wants to write about has disappeared and Ade is convinced that Nwankiti Ogechi has been killed for his pro-democratic beliefs and activism against dictatorship. The other guests try to convince Ade that he should focus on the interview with Big Oga for the time being as the former story is mired in controversy. As soon as Ade gets heated up, Eugene interrupts and leads him away to the study so that they could continue their conversation without making a scene. It was later that evening that the government agents pay a visit to Eugene. On their way out they pull at the hibiscuses as Eugene orders them to leave his house.

The next edition of the *Standard* features Ogechi as the cover story, which is rife with accusations and anger at the murder of such an admirable and innocent individual. Eugene knows that the publishing of such a story is going to have negative consequences; indeed, soon after this story comes out,

Nigeria is suspended from the Commonwealth. As the guests arrive to speak with Eugene, they advise him to be careful and to try and change his work and life routines, lest they should target him and his family for allowing such a story to come out in public. They also warn Eugene by reminding him of those men who were killed even in their own homes for trying to challenge the government.

Jaja, however, is convinced that Eugene is strong and powerful enough to remain unscathed from such violent assaults. Meanwhile, Ifeoma phones Kambili and Jaja to inform them about the funeral being held the following week, and Amaka tells Kambili about her confirmation which is to take place on Easter Sunday, at which Kambili responds that she would be willing to attend. Back in her room, Kambili thinks of Father Amadi and whilst rushing out after, school she remembers what he had told her about her legs being good for running, rather than paying attention to the ridiculing laughter and whispers of 'backyard snob'.

Analysis – section 2 – chapter 9 (pages 162 to 205)

When Ifeoma is worried that her father will want to go back to his rundown hut in his native village, it shows that Papa-Nnukwu is quite headstrong and resilient and would rather succumb to his illness than break his ties with his roots, with the place to which he belongs. This also marks the strength of his traditionalist beliefs and explains his resistance to Eugene's extreme conversion to the Catholic faith. Ifeoma resembles her father in her strength of character and in her willpower to outdo the challenges that she has had to face from the time her husband died. She has yet to face new challenging situations under the new regime and that includes having to find the necessary money to pay off her father's expensive medical bills and medicine. She is not alone in her struggle and her own children prove to be mature beyond their age and with the help of Father Amadi she manages to make it day by day.

Father Amadi comes around quite often in fact and when Kambili excuses herself from going with them to the stadium, he seems determined to make her change her mind. Kambili herself is in an ambivalent situation as she wishes to follow her heart but is too bogged down by what her father expects her to do and by how she is expected to act.

Observing Amaka paint her grandfather, Kambili senses that she is an outsider among them, she feels isolated and pushed away from their special bond. She realises that she has missed out in all these years on having such a relationship like the one Amaka and Papa-Nnukwu share, a relationship based on affection and happiness and not on fear and control as she is accustomed to having with her father. Although a Catholic herself, Ifeoma is open-minded about religion and respects her father's choices instead of expecting him to convert to Catholicism. This is why she tries to convince Kambili that Papa-Nnukwu is not a pagan but he is merely following his traditions; she wants her niece to be tolerant and understanding instead of being brainwashed by her father.

Kambili tries to be more open-minded when she sees her grandfather praying. Even though she is nervous about being in the same room with a 'heathen,' she notices that Papa-Nnukwu was smiling during his prayers and reflects how they hardly ever laughed or smiled, particularly during prayer time. The differences in the children's upbringing become more evident when Kambili is surprised by the casual manner by which Ifeoma, Father Amadi and her cousins hold their conversations without feeling the necessity to weigh every word they utter or ponder any thought that crosses their mind. She admires her cousins Amaka and Obiora for being so outspoken even when challenged by an adult like Father Amadi. When the latter ropes Kambili into the conversation, Amaka scorns her cousin by claiming that Kambili is scared of Father Amadi. The relationship between Kambili and Amaka is still tenuous because the latter insists that Kambili is a spoilt and arrogant daughter of a powerful man.

These arguments between Kambili and Amaka do little to better the situation as the reader is reminded of the harsh conditions under which Ifeoma's family live. Fuel scarcity is further aggravated by a steep rise in the cost of living whereby the basic food items now cost four times more than they used to before the increase in transportation costs. Such a situation is brought on by the inequality of power and the malfunctioning of justice as people struggle to make ends meet. Amidst this upheaval, Father Amadi, Ifeoma and the children have numerous conversations which shed light on pressing issues such as religion, oppression, independence and madness. When one of their talks falls upon Father Amadi's departure to a foreign country, the irony of religion is heightened as one notes how the picture has been reversed: initially the white missionary arrived in 'heathen' countries to convert people to Catholicism and now those same converted Africans were being called upon to go the white man's land to spread God's word in European countries where people were starting to lose faith in God and religion.

Papa-Nnukwu cannot understand why Father Amadi is needed in the white man's land but he tries to advise Father Amadi to do anything but lie to the people as the white missionaries have done in order to lure his son away from him. Unfortunately Father Amadi knows that priests might sometimes resort to lying so that people might see the light and accept religion and God into their lives. From his personal experience, Papa-Nnukwu has had to lose his son to religion and still cannot accept how this new religion tolerated such a son's disrespect for his elders.

When Father Amadi finally convinces Kambili to go to the stadium with him, she is concerned about wearing shorts because her father had rigorously taught her that looking at oneself in the mirror was sinful and therefore wearing revealing clothes was not allowed because it would inevitably lead to that kind of temptation. The fact that Kambili tries to wear lipstick, however, indicates that she is becoming more aware of her feminine side and self-confident about adapting to new situations. Father Amadi's keen sense of observation picks up on the tiniest of details and he notices the lipstick mark on Kambili's hand; she is pleased that he is aware of her effort to wear lipstick for the first time and this makes her smile, not once but twice, which is no mean feat for Kambili was not at all used to smiling so instinctively and openly. Father Amadi's influence on Kambili is staggering for not only does he make her change her attitude (particularly towards her grandfather) and bring out her personality but he also helps her discover the woman that lies inside her. In her turn, Kambili feels comfortable in Father Amadi's presence even though excited by the prospect of being alone with him.

When they talk about Papa-Nnuwku, religion and her father, Kambili feels slightly ill at ease when she realises that Jaja has told Father Amadi things that they should never talk about. This means that Jaja is changing and it helps to explain why the novel starts off with Jaja's refusal to receive Holy Communion and to practise religion after his stay at Nsukka. Kambili's transformation does not run parallel to that of her brother, however, and Father Amadi picks up on this when he realises that Kambili is still heavily dictated by what her father thinks, believes and expects her to do. She is totally afraid of her father and Father Amadi tries to loosen her up by not only taking her to the stadium but asking her to participate. Kambili's strict upbringing, however, impedes her from playing – from a very early age, she was meant to follow tight schedules and this explains why she has had hardly any time to practise sports of any sort.

She cannot cope with running after Father Amadi, in fact, but this chasing game of his helps her realise that she needs to find her freedom and spirituality rather than blindly adhering to one that is imposed by her father. The fact that Father Amadi congratulates her on her legs boosts Kambili's confidence immensely and the comment 'you have good legs for running' will remain etched in her memory for a long time.

Kambili notices that it is Father Amadi's nature to spark young people's confidence, like he does with the boys at the stadium. When Father Amadi talks about them, Kambili realises that she has always lived a sheltered life, unlike these boys who have had to give up their education and seek meagre employment due to the political turmoil. Kambili is surprised by their positive attitude in spite of their shabby clothes and lack of basic amenities. This shows that people learn to make do and appreciate what they have.

When Papa-Nnukwu passes away, everyone is saddened but Kambili is even more shocked by her brother's unbecoming behaviour when he approaches Papa-Nnukwu's dead body. She cannot understand that, unlike her, Jaja has become more audacious and is not afraid of what his father might say or do. When Eugene arrives unannounced, he does not offer any condolences for his father's death in fact. He is very insensitive when he voices his anger at not being informed immediately that his children had been staying with Papa-Nnukwu, and his insensitivity is even more pronounced when he refuses to fund the funeral unless his father is converted; this underlines his religious stubbornness and marks the ongoing conflicts between brother and sister.

These conflicts demonstrate how confident and strong Ifeoma is in spite of her brother's equally imposing character. The fact that he eventually gives in and agrees to pay for the funeral shows how important it was for Ifeoma to stand up to him and not to surrender to his will. Unfortunately, the people in Nigeria are unwilling to stand up to their corrupt government as they are afraid of the consequences.

In spite of having changed his mind about the funeral, Eugene is not willing to forgive his children because he expected them to phone him and inform him about Papa-Nnukwu. The fact that Eugene punishes Jaja and Kambili in the same way he had been punished as a young boy shows that his way of pursuing religion is overly puritanical and that it is a vicious circle whereby the same methods of punishment are inflicted upon the sinner, generation after generation.

It is religion taken to an extreme where corporal punishments are reminiscent of the torture carried out by harsh religious orders such as the Inquisition. Kambili's reaction to her punishment, however, is unexpected as she does not seem to give in to the pain inflicted by the boiling water; that she thinks of her grandfather and of Amaka's portrait marks a radical change in Kambili. This can also mean that she is not frightened of her father as she used to be before Nsukka. Amaka's gesture – of having given Kambili the portrait as a present –shows that she too is undergoing a change of heart towards her cousin; it means that she is starting to warm up to Kambili and is more tolerant of the differences between them. While Kambili is excited over her secret present, Jaja is also thrilled by the idea of planting the purple hibiscus stalks – the fact that they are deliberately hiding something from their father means that Nsukka has changed them and made them both more daring, even though Jaja is more audacious than his sister.

Eugene has other problems to contend with such as problems at the *Standard*. Since freedom of expression is prohibited under the dictatorial regime, only politically correct news stories are advised. Ade Coker's insistence that he prints the Ogechi story underscores the courage that some men still possess in a country where people are afraid to speak out against the injustices committed by a corrupt regime. The other writers, however, are more cautious and it seems that Coker's arrest has not deterred him from being a frontrunner for justice. Ogechi's own death at the hands of the military has already shown how democracy is repressed and quashed by dictatorship. It is ironic therefore that Eugene attempts to fight off the injustice and dictatorship when his own children have to struggle against his own mini-dictatorship set up within the strong walls of his house.

Synopsis – section 2 – chapter 10 (pages 206 to 216)

Eugene and his family learn about the shocking death of Ade Coker, who is killed by a letter bomb which he opens in front of his family during breakfast. Ade's family is traumatised by the accident and Eugene feels guilty of being responsible for his friend's death as he did nothing to stop Ade from holding back the controversial story of Ogechi. Beatrice and his children are very supportive and reassure him that he is not to blame. To compensate, Eugene arranges for Ade's funeral to be held and offers a trust fund and a new house to Yewande Coker and her children. He also decides to send his staff of the *Standard* on leave and pays them huge bonuses. Kambili starts to have nightmares of her father being blown up in the same way as Ade.

The death of Ade Coker takes a heavy toll on Eugene, particularly after the soldiers close down one of his factories by claiming that there were rats. As a result, Eugene stops going to the other factories and stays at home for longer periods, not even bothering to check whether his children are following their schedules. Kambili and Jaja take advantage of his longer absences when Jaja asks his sister to show him Papa-Nnukwu's portrait; reluctant at first, Kambili relents but just as they are intently staring at it, Eugene walks in and is clearly shocked by what he sees. When Eugene asks to whom it belongs, both

Kambili and Jaja admit to it being theirs; enraged, Eugene tears it to pieces and as Kambili crouches on the ground to save what she can, her father begins kicking her violently until she loses consciousness.

The next time Kambili awakens she realises she is in hospital and, half-dazed from the injections, she picks up some words that reflect her injuries: broken rib, internal bleeding. Her parents are by her side. Even though it was her father who brought this upon her, he utters words of love and cannot stop crying. Father Benedict also visits to give her extreme unction, but she hears her mother reassure her that it is not that serious. Kambili asks her mother to contact Ifeoma. The latter comes along with Father Amadi, and Kambili recognises their voices, as she is still feeling dizzy from all the medications. Ifeoma scolds Beatrice for letting such a thing happen and she insists that as soon as Kambili is out of hospital, they should all leave Eugene.

Eugene hires a private tutor for Kambili to resume her studies as soon as she feels better; a young Reverend Sister gives Kambili lessons, using English for teaching and sometimes Igbo for talking about other things. Kambili sits for exams in hospital and even finishes early; when the results are out, Kambili learns that she has placed first. Beatrice is elated. That same afternoon, Kambili's classmates visit her and they are all in awe of her for having survived what they were told was a terrible accident. Even Chinwe Jideze, her sworn competitor, comes along and gives her a card with 'Get well to someone special' on it. As soon as Kambili leaves hospital, they leave for Nsukka as Eugene is convinced that a change of air would help her recovery.

Analysis – section 2 – chapter 10 (pages 206 to 216)

Ade Coker's courage and determination to speak out against the injustices of the military regime are severely punished when he is killed by a letter bomb. The government does not even try to hide the truth because there is the government seal on the letter; it is an open and clear warning of what happens to those who meddle with the truth. In spite of being strong and confident, Eugene cannot cope with Ade's death. He does not know how to channel his frustration and anger and when he discovers that Kambili and Jaja had kept Papa-Nnukwu's portrait a secret and that they were having fun watching a 'heathen's' face, he takes it out on them. It is a vicious circle where the ones who are hurt beat up those who are weaker, and it is shameful to see that Eugene engenders more violence instead of protecting his family from further violence.

His violence lands Kambili in hospital, fighting for her life. The fact that Kambili studies, sits for her exams and places first while in hospital shows how Kambili has succeeded in nurturing a strong character and self-confidence even though she is still wary of her father. However, Father Amadi's presence has left an indelible mark on Kambili's character so much that she demands her mother to phone Ifeoma, who is incensed at Beatrice for lacking the willpower and courage to correct her husband's ways; in fact, she reminds one of the weak people who are left behind in Nigeria to succumb to the dictatorship. So whereas everyone is changing, including Kambili who shows amazing strength to outdo the odds against her, Beatrice is the only character who remains constant and passive, unwilling and unable to change.

Synopsis – section 2 – chapter 11 (pages 217 to 239)

Kambili's recovery in Nsukka is aided by her cousins' help who insist on doing things for her, as they are afraid she would exert herself unnecessarily. Ifeoma does not tell them what happened but lets them know that Kambili had nearly died.

Kambili feels more at ease with Amaka, who teases her about being Father Amadi's 'sweetheart'. She informs Kambili that he is indeed very concerned about her and Kambili admits to having a 'crush' on him, like the other girls on campus and even married women. Kambili is taken unawares when Amaka claims that it was Uncle Eugene who hit her so badly; for the first time, Kambili admits the truth.

That evening there is a blackout once again and Father Amadi comes over to see how Kambili is faring. Kambili wishes she were alone with Father Amadi, who entertains them with his childhood stories. The next day, a woman from the university comes over to inform Ifeoma that the university governing council is being replaced by a sole administrator. As Ifeoma is shocked by this, the woman gives her more bad news: there is a list of lecturers who have been accused of disloyalty to the government and that Ifeoma's name is on it; this would result in these lecturers being fired.

Ifeoma is furious about this matter and she claims that she has always spoken the truth. Ifeoma is afraid that students and lecturers alike will soon be threatened by the soldiers into accepting what is demanded of them. Ifeoma's colleague offers to drop her off for her lecture; meanwhile, Amaka and Obiora fill Kambili in on the details: the democratic council has been replaced by a sole administrator who will be responsible for major and minor decisions at the university. Obiora and Amaka discuss their other option: that of going to America where their mother can work undisturbed, instead of being threatened and being denied the promotion to senior lecturer. Kambili is sad to hear about the possibility of her aunty and cousins leaving for America.

That same evening, Father Amadi comes over to take them all to the stadium. Amaka teases him that he is only interested in Kambili and as a result only she goes with him. Father

Amadi trains the boys to jump over obstacles, and as they are distracted, he pulls up the rod slightly so that they are made to jump higher. He then suggests that Kambili's hair should be plaited and offers to take her to her aunty's hairdresser. As he lightly touches her hair, Kambili wishes she could show him the warmth that his touch has engendered.

The next morning, Amaka wakes Kambili up to the noise of the students' riots going on in the street. They hurry to turn off the lights in case the rioters might be tempted to hurl stones at the windows. Ifeoma reassures Kambili that they are safe even though during the previous riot, the students set fire to a senior professor's car. They soon find out that the students are protesting against the sole administrator and the Head of State who imposed this upon the university. When Ifeoma returns with news of the riot, they learn that this riot was the worst one as the students burnt down the sole administrator's house, along with six university cars. The sole administrator and his wife manage to escape and the university is closed down due to the unrest. In one of her nightmares, Kambili dreams that the sole administrator is pouring boiling water over her aunty's feet and that she flies out of the bathtub into America.

That evening, Ifeoma and the children are disturbed by four agents from the special security unit who burst loudly into Ifeoma's flat; they demand to search the place as they accuse her of collaborating with the rioters and trying to sabotage the peace of the university. As she angrily demands an explanation for this sudden intrusion, Obiora tries to act manly by questioning them too until Ifeoma asks him and the others to sit quietly until the men leave. Before they do so, the men point their finger at Ifeoma and warn her to be very careful. When they leave, Ifeoma knows it is useless to contact the police station, because these men are in collaboration with the police force. Obiora insists that they should leave and that

Ifeoma should contact Phillipa for them to go to America. Amaka is not convinced that leaving is the best solution but Obiora believes they have no other choice.

Whilst they are having breakfast the following morning, Amaka complains about the homemade soybean milk and Ifeoma explains that even dried milk is too expensive. Just then, one of Ifeoma's students arrives, bringing a chicken with her to announce her marriage. The student informs Ifeoma that she is leaving university because now that it has been closed down, her fiancé is not willing to wait any longer and she has no choice but to give up her education in order to get married and to have children, as everyone expects her to do.

Jaja offers to kill the chicken and Kambili is surprised that he is capable of doing such a thing. She observes him as he kills the chicken with a single-minded and cold precision and she realises how much Jaja has changed throughout their stays at Nsukka. Jaja tells Kambili that he is determined to leave with his aunty and cousins should they decide to go to America. Kambili remains silent at this comment and notices the vultures hovering above, waiting to eat the chicken's entrails; Amaka remembers Papa-Nnukwu saying that when the vultures came down to eat the entrails, it meant the gods were pleased. Father Amadi stops by to inform Ifeoma that he is taking Kambili to have her hair plaited.

When Kambili goes with Father Amadi to Mama Joe's shed in Ogige market to have her hair plaited, she is welcomed by the women there. Mama Joe enquires how Ifeoma is coping these days and admires her for being such a strong woman.

Mama Joe at first thinks that Father Amadi is Kambili's brother but upon being told that he is a priest, she is surprised because she has noticed the way he looks at Kambili. She also tells Kambili that usually men bring the women they love to have their hair plaited. Kambili does not know how to respond to such a comment. On their way home, Father Amadi comments on how different and how much better Kambili looks now that her hair has been plaited and he suggests that she should play the part of Our Lady in their play. When she replies that she does not know how to act, he encourages her by stating that she could do whatever she wanted. Kambili then starts singing Igbo choruses along with Father Amadi.

Analysis – section 2 – chapter 11 (pages 217 to 239)

Amaka has changed towards Kambili; she is more supportive and teases in a friendly manner. Unlike Kambili, Amaka is not afraid to face the truth, even though it is unpleasant at times. By letting Kambili know that she is aware of how the injuries came about, Amaka shows maturity beyond her years. Even when faced with daily problems, such as power cuts, Amaka and her brothers, stand up to fear and with the ongoing support of their mother and Father Amadi, they pull through many difficult situations.

Ifeoma's strength is sorely tested when she hears about the infamous list and that she is amongst the lecturers who risk losing their job. However, she remains bold in order to set a good example for her children. Even so, she is powerless against the changes at the workplace, particularly when the sole administrator is the voice for the dictatorial head of state. So anyone who speaks against the way things are conducted will risk being fired; this includes Ifeoma, who is being warned to hold her tongue if she does not wish to be accused of disloyalty.

The alternative of emigrating to America or to other countries has been a reality that many people have had to face since the independence of many African states from the British Empire, particularly when these Free states started descending into chaos after having been taken over by dictatorial leaders. Obiora and Amaka do not share the same views regarding emigration.

Amaka scolds her brother by explaining that by escaping he is not going to solve anything and that strong people like them should stay around to fix things. Obiora insists that there is nothing else left for them here and that they won't be able to pursue their studies once all the good professors will have left. Amaka and Obiora's conversation reflects that of many Africans who are uprooted involuntarily from their native country. However, Ifeoma and her family seem to have no choice other than that of leaving because they are continuously threatened; after the agents from the special unit barge in on Ifeoma warning her against shady dealings, she decides that it is not safe for them to stay behind. The fact that they cannot even report the incident to the police shows that corruption is rampant particularly in the higher echelons of the country.

Meanwhile, at the stadium, Father Amadi explains to Kambili that with the right dose of encouragement, young people like her can be helped to aim higher and be more self-confident. She then realises that Ifeoma adopts the same attitude with her children, encouraging them to strive for the best. Kambili is impressed by the way Father Amadi places his trust in these boys and he explains that he needs to believe in things that do not need to be questioned. The fact that Father Amadi takes Kambili to plait her hair shows that he respects her, especially when Kambili is told that a man who brings a woman to do her hair does so out of love. Father Amadi's gesture is ambiguous because Kambili cannot understand his motivations, other than wanting to help her become more confident and aware of her hidden beauty. The fact that she starts singing with Father Amadi on their way home means that he is succeeding in bringing the shy Kambili out of her shell and he instils further confidence in her when he suggests that she can undertake anything she wishes to; even though there is an element of exaggeration in that comment, it lifts Kambili's spirits and makes her feel special.

Synopsis – section 2 – chapter 12 (pages 240 to 253)

Kambili attends church with Ifeoma and her children. Father Amadi comes over to discuss Amaka's English name that she is meant to choose for her confirmation ceremony. Amaka, however, does not see the point in doing so even though Father Amadi offers to help her choose one. Ifeoma tells her friend Chiaku about the security agents and they discuss the latest incident at university: how Professor Okafor's son was caught stealing the exam papers and selling them to the students; consequently, Okafor beat his son even though he was one of the corrupt professors who created the list of disloyal lecturers. They talk about America and how Phillipa has succeeded in starting a new life there, even though Chiaku does not believe that people like them are respected in the white man's land. When Obiora offers his opinion, he berates Chiaku for talking nonsense and Ifeoma sends him to his room to wait for his punishment: a light flogging followed by a talk.

Kambili comments about having to waste so much meat but Ifeoma shows her how she preserves it and Amaka jokes about Kambili being a Big Man's daughter. As they hear the sound of a car approaching, they realise it is Beatrice. They are shocked to see her all dishevelled and looking strained. They find out that Beatrice has just come from hospital where she has had another miscarriage (she was six weeks pregnant) after her husband broke the table where they kept the family Bible on her belly. Ifeoma is outraged and does not allow Beatrice to speak to Eugene over the phone. Beatrice excuses her husband for such behaviour but Ifeoma is not willing to forgive Eugene for such an act. Amaka, however, understands that certain people, including her uncle, have different ways of dealing with stress.

Eugene comes to pick them up and Kambili notices how his face had become clouded with rashes even though he puts it down to some allergy. Kambili does not hug her father but instead salutes Amaka, who hugs her and addresses her as *nwanne m nwanyi*, my sister. Making eye contact with Jaja, Kambili wishes she could stay behind to spend Easter with her aunty and cousins, to attend Amaka's confirmation, and to sing during Father Amadi's Pascal Mass. When they arrive in Enugu, Jaja observes how the purple hibiscuses are soon going to blossom. Kambili reflects how the following day was Palm Sunday, the day in which Jaja refuses to receive communion and Eugene throws the missal at him and breaks Beatrice's figurines.

Analysis – section 2 – chapter 12 (pages 240 to 253)

When Kambili attends church at Nsukka, she notices that the women there do not make such a fuss over what they wear for church and she reflects how her father would be irritated that women would wear jeans or not tie up their hair in the scarf properly. This indicates that she is still in awe of her father and that her thoughts are aligned with his. It also shows how strict Eugene is in how women dress and this explains why Kambili was not used to wearing shorts or baring her legs in any other way.

Both Ifeoma and Chiaku agree that corruption starts from the higher ranks and that as a result the children end up rebelling or changing so drastically that their own parents are unable to recognise them. They also mention Phillipa and whereas Ifeoma is tempted to join her friend in America, Chiaku is more sceptical and warns Ifeoma that people like them are treated like second-rate citizens and have to accept menial jobs instead of being offered the work that they have been trained in, so that lawyers and doctors have to drive taxis or wash plates. Ifeoma is concerned about her children and knows that they face a grim future if there is nobody to teach them at university.

When Chiaku tries to convince Ifeoma that leaving the weak ones to break the cycle will only help to increase the corruption, Obiora opines that Chiaku is not being realistic. Ifeoma is clearly irritated by Obiora's arrogance and later she argues with him not for having expressed his opinion but for the way in which he has insulted her friend. Whilst Ifeoma is lecturing Obiora, Amaka explains to Kambili that their mother's 'punishments' come in the form of long talks, even after she flogs them. This shows that Ifeoma does not adopt the same measures of punishment that Eugene is accustomed to using; there is more respect towards her children even though she does punish them. She acknowledges, however, that they can learn from their mistakes by talking about it rather than by punishing them harshly and instilling fear in them like Eugene does with Kambili and Jaja.

When Beatrice arrives surprising and shocking everyone simultaneously, it shows that she has made an effort to stand up to Eugene for once, to speak out against him and to say the truth. However, Ifeoma still cannot understand why Beatrice constantly forgives Eugene, especially when she excuses him for having brought on another miscarriage, explaining that he has been quite stressed lately and has been shouldering other people's problems apart from his own. For Ifeoma, this is inexcusable and mentions how her own husband had never hit her even when they faced a crisis. Beatrice insists on covering up for him by admitting that she is afraid that the village people will succeed in marrying him off to one of the much younger women. Ifeoma cannot accept that excuse for such behaviour. Surprisingly, however, Amaka reflects that Uncle Eugene is just a man with many problems and he makes mistakes because he might not know how to cope when placed under pressure; she also adds that he did after all pay for her grandfather's funeral. Kambili dreads the thought of going back to Enugu but her mother insists they leave immediately.

When Eugene comes to take them home, Kambili refrains from hugging him; this shows that she is not afraid as she used to be. The fact that Kambili says her goodbyes to her cousins, shows that she has forged a new and healthier relationship with them, especially with Amaka, who even shows a marked improvement when she calls Kambili 'my sister.' Back home, Kambili's story comes full circle when she comments on how Jaja does not receive communion and this action is just the beginning of a downward turn of events for Eugene and his family.

The Pieces of Gods
– After Palm Sunday

Synopsis – section 3 – chapter 1
(pages 257 to 270)

Kambili observes the devastating effect of the bad weather on their surroundings, and indoors too a number of things get broken, one of them being Beatrice's china set. She feels an odd silence looming above them and notices how Beatrice too is changing, seemingly not afraid of doing certain things in front of her husband, such as taking the food up to Jaja's room. Kambili hears her father ask Jaja to eat with them in the evening but Jaja refuses to do so. Meanwhile, Yewande Coker pays Eugene a visit to inform him that things are getting better at home; her daughter has started speaking again with the help of Eugene, who had paid for the best doctors and for Yewande to take her daughter abroad. Whilst Eugene is in the study praying, Kambili informs Jaja about Yewande and her family.

When Easter Sunday approaches, Kambili is worried about what would happen if Jaja refuses to go to communion. On Good Friday, Ifeoma phones and Eugene decides to go to evening mass because he is not feeling well. Kambili speaks to Ifeoma, who tells her that her children, Father Amadi and herself, are all leaving the country. Her aunty informs her that she has no choice but to leave for America because she been fired. She tells Kambili that she has applied for a visa at the American Embassy, and that Father Amadi has been chosen to go to Germany at the end of the month. At this news, Jaja decides to leave for Nsukka so as to spend Easter with his aunty and cousins, and he is even willing to walk there if he has to. Realising that he is now powerless against his son, Eugene relents and asks Kevin to drive them, although Kevin in concerned about Eugene being unable to drive to church as he is not well enough. As they say goodbye to their parents, Kambili reassures her father that it will not be long before they return to Enugu.

At Nsukka, the conversation inevitably turns to Ifeoma and her children's imminent departure to America. Obiora suggests that they could use all of the gas in the cooker because they will soon be leaving. Amaka, however, tells him not to be so impulsive because their mother has not been granted the visa yet and it is very difficult for Nigerian people to get their visas approved. Nonetheless, Obiora is hopeful that being sponsored by a university will speed things up for them. Amaka senses that Kambili is not comfortable listening to their conversation about leaving so she changes the subject by telling her that Papa-Nnukwu always told them that a blazing sun during the rainy season means that it will rain soon. When Father Amadi comes around to see how everyone is doing, Obiora notes how the priest comes more often when Kambili is at Nsukka. Kambili's cousins are sad to see their favourite priest leave and Amaka comments on how a black priest like Father Amadi is taking the Catholic God back to the white man's land. Father Amadi explains that he is just a missionary of God who has the duty to strengthen religion in those countries that are fast losing priests.

When Father Amadi notices that Kambili has been particularly silent from the moment he arrived, he reassures her that whatever she thinks and feels will always be important to him. She tells him that her father phoned but that neither she nor Jaja spoke to him, even though she wanted to. She confides in Father Amadi that she is concerned about him and Ifeoma leaving at the same time and that she and Jaja will be all alone once school begins. Father Amadi, however, informs her that he has spoken to Ifeoma about this problem and that it will be best for Kambili and Jaja to attend boarding school once he and Father Benedict will have convinced Eugene. Kambili feels much better that Father Amadi has taken their interests seriously. That same night, Kambili bathes and sings but does not wash her left hand which Father Amadi had held gently to slide the flower off her finger.

Analysis – section 3 – chapter 1 (pages 257 to 270)

Bad weather takes a toll on Kambili's house and the surroundings and inside their house things are changing too. In an example of pathetic fallacy, the breakages brought about by bad weather seem to complement the breaking up of the family fabric as things start to fall apart, bringing us back to the first section of the novel. The fact that Beatrice has finally shown the willingness to change towards her husband, in doing things without being afraid of him, indicates that the sooner she stands up to Eugene, as Jaja has started to do before her, the sooner will her family be rid of his strict and unendurable regime. It seems ironic that the same man who has always threatened the safety of his own family's wellbeing could be capable of performing benevolent acts towards others, such as helping Yewande Coker after the death of Ade.

This has always been a contradictory aspect of Eugene's character and it might be that Beatrice and her family always kept the truth hidden in order not to tarnish Eugene's reputation as a pillar of their community. In fact, Eugene being a benefactor of other families does not mean that he has changed his attitude and behaviour towards his own. Even though he has mellowed down, it is because he has lost the drive to follow up on things and because he has realised that his children and wife are not afraid of him anymore and not because he has finally accepted that his methods were inhumane. So when Eugene agrees to pay for the best doctors for Yewande's daughter and for many other good causes since Ade's demise, he does it mostly out of guilt and anger at himself than out of pity for other people. Jaja is realistic and cynical as he ascertains that no amount of money will guarantee that Yewande's daughter will recover fully from the psychological trauma even though she has started speaking.

Kambili is still anxious about what her father might do if Jaja decides to renounce his faith but is more shocked to learn of the confirmed departure of her aunty, cousins and Father Amadi. She is afraid of being left alone by the only people who have given her a true home in the last months and she cannot imagine her future without them. Jaja is also saddened by this news but this emboldens him to take the decision to go to Nsukka immediately. The fact that he does not ask his father's permission shows that he has taken the role of the man of the house upon himself; he feels independent and is capable of resisting his father's rules. In fact, Eugene accepts without questioning or scolding Jaja and this indicates that it is Eugene who is almost in awe of his son. Jaja seems to be repeating the cycle of father-son behaviour: as Eugene has lost his respect towards his father on account of religious differences, Jaja seems to have lost his respect towards his father on realising what a dictator Eugene is and on refusing to follow his orders any longer. He does not even say goodbye to his father and this is an indication of his strength and insensitivity towards his father, whereas Kambili still cannot leave without reassuring her father and showing deep empathy towards him.

When they arrive at Nsukka, one can feel the tension as everyone awaits news of Ifeoma's visa. Amaka does not really want to leave and does not believe that her mother will be granted the visa as easily as Obiora would like to believe; Amaka knows that the corruption and lack of justice in their country will make it harder for their mother to achieve such an invaluable document. Obiora is excited and hopeful that with the university's sponsorship his mother will succeed. Kambili feels isolated from their conversation and even when Father Amadi drops by, she is awfully morose. Her silence allows her to deal with the emotional turmoil, and she feels wary of his empty promises and false hopes when Father Amadi tries to reassure her that she will always be important to him. The only thing that sounds reassuring is that he will take responsibility for Jaja and Kambili's wellbeing by entrusting them to a boarding school. Whether or not this promise will be fulfilled is yet to be seen. Meanwhile, Kambili is still deeply infatuated by Father Amadi as she does not wash the spot where his fingers touched her hand.

Synopsis – section 3 – chapter 2 (pages 271 to 287)

Father Amadi stops by to help Amaka choose an English name, but she adamantly refuses to do so as she feels that it is a thing of the past, a tradition that was common when the missionaries first came. Father Amadi tries to convince her that it is just a formality and that nobody is forced to use it. When Amaka insists on refusing, Ifeoma shouts at her and demands that in order for her to get confirmed she has to choose a name. By Easter Sunday, however, Amaka had still not given in and whereas all the other children had pieces of paper with their English names written on them, Amaka was the odd one out who did not join the naming ceremony.

Ifeoma decides that it is time they all went on the pilgrimage to Aokpe, probably because she knew that it would be a very long time before they would return to Nigeria, especially as her visa had been approved. Jaja refuses to go and Obiora and Chima decide to stay behind too. Since Ifeoma would have liked to be accompanied by a male, she asks Father Amadi to go with them. Amaka knows that Father Amadi will definitely agree to go with them on account of Kambili being there. She is proved right as Father Amadi, Ifeoma, Kambili and Amaka set off for the pilgrimage where they encounter hundreds of cars and multitudes of people who were packed so closely that they all blended into one huge crowd. Kambili is mesmerised by this scene when Amaka comments on how she will always remember Aokpe not for the alleged apparitions but for bringing Kambili and Jaja to them. When Father Amadi questions whether Amaka believes in the apparition, Kambili blurts out that she felt the Blessed Virgin's presence and Father Amadi agrees that something godly had taken place there.

Kambili accompanies Father Amadi on campus to say goodbye to the other families before his departure. Everywhere he went people were sad to see him leave and whilst in the car, Kambili plucks up enough courage to declare that she loves him. He looks at Kambili and with saddened eyes tells her that she is very young and that she will find more love in the lifetime that awaits her. Kambili inwardly does not believe what he has just told her and when she arrives at Nsukka she brushes off Ifeoma's questions with indifference. Ifeoma asks Kambili to pray that her visa application would be approved but Kambili felt that doing so would mean losing her aunty and cousins apart from losing Father Amadi. Kambili finds Amaka in her bedroom. Kambili starts singing along to the tunes of Amaka's music and the latter is surprised by this. Suddenly Amaka feels sad because she knows that in America she would not be able to find her favourite musician's tapes. Kambili does not answer her question for she is afraid she might give her cousin the wrong impression; she does not want Amaka to think that she wants them to leave.

Kambili feels agitated when Ifeoma comes back from Lagos with news about the visa; her fears are justified when Ifeoma informs them that she has got the visa. Obiora is overjoyed but Kambili, Amaka and Jaja are not too pleased. Ifeoma explains how difficult it is to get a visa and tells them about countless other people being refused one, even if they are just going for a short stay. She feels the people are treated like footballs and that they grant a person a visa depending on their mood. Ifeoma informs them that they have two weeks to vacate the flat and that during that time she will have to find the money for the flights. She will have to swallow her pride and ask Eugene to help and at the same time she will tell him about Jaja and Kambili attending boarding school. Ifeoma, Father Amadi and Father Benedict all believe that it is the best thing for Kambili and Jaja.

Father Amadi's last day also approaches and Kambili prefers not to accompany him on his final errands for it is too painful for her to bear. When Kambili asks him about what had motivated him to take her to the stadium, he admits that at first it was to please Ifeoma but after the first time, he felt he wanted to take her every day. Kambili refuses to look at him and he leaves, promising to return in the evening.

Amaka teases Kambili that there is something almost sexual going on between her and Father Amadi. She even suggests that they should offer optional celibacy in the priesthood so that Kambili might have a chance with Father Amadi; Kambili is not amused by Amaka's jokes because she knows well he will never leave the priesthood for her. She does however take note of Father Amadi's German address and he promises to write first. That night, after dinner, Kambili dreams that she is running down a rocky path with Father Amadi chasing her and then her father continues to chase her; she wishes to tell Amaka about it but instead allows her cousin to hold her and lull her to sleep.

After they pack all their belongings, Ifeoma proposes going for a drive around Nsukka for the last time. Kambili wishes that something would happen, that something would change, such as Father Amadi returning to her. As they stop at the foot of Odim hill, Ifeoma suggests they climb to the top and Obiora comes up with the idea of picnicking on the hillside. They all run to the top. Running reminds Kambili of Father Amadi looking at her legs and Amaka in fact hints that Kambili should try training to become a sprinter. Everyone laughs wholeheartedly and Kambili realises how easy laughing had become. On their way down, however, Kambili loses hope of seeing Father Amadi turn up.

That evening, the phone rings and as the TV was off, Kambili could clearly discern her aunty's scream. Sensing that something bad must have happened, they all rush to her and when Kambili speaks to her mother, she learns that her father had been found dead on his desk at the factory. At first Kambili suspects it to have been a letter bomb and then she realises that she always thought her father was immortal, that she had never envisaged the possibility of him being killed.

Analysis – section 3 – chapter 2 (pages 271 to 287)

Amaka's stubbornness at not wanting to choose an English name shows how respectful she is of her African name and of their traditions which have been instilled into her by Papa-Nnukwu. Even though Father Amadi insists on her choosing an English name for her confirmation, he assures her that it is just a formality and he himself does not use his English name but has retained his native one. This shows how tolerant and open he is towards people of different beliefs.

Even though Ifeoma tries to convince Amaka to do as they advise her to, she finally accepts that Amaka can make her own decisions and does not scold or punish her when Amaka has her way, even though she is the only girl not to participate in the ceremony. Similarly, Jaja is adamant when it comes to religion; his attitude has changed so drastically towards the Catholic faith that he refuses to accompany them on the pilgrimage to Aokpe. However, this pilgrimage is special for Amaka who believes it is what brought her cousins to Nsukka; it is special also for Kambili as she gets the last chance to spend more time with her aunty, Amaka and Father Amadi before they leave. Although Father Amadi and Amaka seem sceptical about the apparition, Kambili believes something magical has happened in Aokpe. Thus, whereas Jaja has lost his faith in religion, Kambili has strengthened hers during her coming-of-age journey.

Kambili does not take Father Amadi's departure very well and this is evident in her refusal to accompany him on his final errands. She wishes she could be angrier at him so that she would not feel the urge to cry. This indicates that Kambili looks at Father Amadi as though he were her lover, as though he were leaving her for another cause. In fact, Amaka and Obiora sense that there is a spiritual and almost sexual bond between Kambili and Father Amadi. Kambili knows, however, that he will never renounce the priesthood. When Father Amadi holds Kambili in his arms she will remember as one of the happiest and saddest moments in her life. Kambili's dream of being chased by Father Amadi and by her father indicates that there is more sorrow to come (Father Amadi leaves and her father dies).

In fact, as Kambili wonders whether her dream was predictive of something big that would happen and she wishes, for a moment, that it would be for the best, that Father Amadi would come back. This is because she cannot imagine her life without him and without her aunty and cousins. Nor could she have ever imagined her father being capable of dying when she finds out about it over the phone. There is something strange when Beatrice phones and gives them the news quite coldly, devoid of emotion. This is confirmed when she informs them that it was she who had poisoned him. This indicates the end of an era, Eugene's era, and from this moment onwards, all is bound to change. Does this mean that Kambili and Jaja are entirely free? Does it mean that losing a father will enable Kambili to feel better?

Synopsis – section 3 – chapter 3 (pages 288 to 291)

Back home, Jaja and Kambili sit with their mother in the living room. Beatrice had locked the gates and instructed Adamu not to allow anyone to visit or offer their condolences. Everyone else feels it was unusual to turn people away but Beatrice insisted on mourning privately and that if people wanted they could offer masses for Eugene's soul. Being older than his cousin, Jaja feels guilty but Kambili tries to persuade him that he is not to blame for what was happening and when Kambili mentions how God works in mysterious ways, Jaja angrily responds that God is truly mysterious as he allowed his son to die instead of saving the people himself.

Kambili wishes that her father was still alive for her to hear his voice, but Jaja does not answer when she wonders how St Agnes would be full of people. Their conversation is interrupted by the incessant ringing of the phone and soon after they learn that their father had been poisoned. Beatrice confesses that she had put poison in his tea. When the policemen come over to enquire about Eugene's death, Jaja immediately confesses that he had killed his father and explains how he had poured rat poison in his tea. He is then arrested.

Analysis – section 3 – chapter 3 (pages 288 to 291)

When they return to Enugu, Jaja feels guilty at not having been there for his mother, like Obiora who is responsible for Aunty Ifeoma's family. When Kambili tries to comfort Jaja, he retorts that God should be held accountable for having killed his own son. Jaja cannot tolerate the injustices of the world; he cannot excuse what happens by accepting that God works in mysterious ways.

When Jaja admits that he could have done more for his mother, it is as though he knew all along that she would kill her husband. Kambili is speechless to hear this news not only because her mother had poisoned him but mostly because she had put it in his tea, which had always been a sign of their family love. When the policemen come to arrest Beatrice, Jaja once again takes the blame by claiming responsibility for the murder. While Jaja questions why God had to kill his son for mankind to be saved, he ironically does the same thing for his mother, that is, he sacrifices himself for her to be saved. Jaja's defiant behaviour towards his father is hence replaced with devotion and responsibility towards his mother and sister. With this incident, Adichie closes the penultimate section.

A Different Silence
– The Present

Synopsis – Epilogue (pages 295 to 307)

Kambili and Beatrice regularly visit Jaja in prison and they are always told that his release is imminent, only to have their hopes dashed every time and his sentence prolonged. On their way to prison, Kambili notices how her mother had stopped caring about her appearance, how she looked like one of the mad and dishevelled women in Ogbete market. When Beatrice insists on telling people that it was she who had poisoned her husband, people start to believe that she is fast losing her mind and that she is constantly living in a state of grief for her husband's death and denial in being unable to accept her son's imprisonment.

There is a new silence between mother and daughter and Kambili reflects on how there are many things they do not talk about, such as financial matters, bribing policemen, judges and prison guards, and Eugene's huge donations to numerous charities and hospitals. In prison, conditions are harsh and rough and consequently, Jaja is quickly growing into a hardened man who shows no emotions and has no hope of being released any time soon, his official status being 'Awaiting Trial'. Kambili notes the physical changes in her brother too.

Kambili decides to go back to Nsukka and upon knocking on the door that was once Ifeoma's flat, she is greeted by a new family who nonetheless invites her in for a glass of water. Meanwhile, Amaka writes long letters, informing Kambili that Ifeoma is working at a community college and at a pharmacy. She also writes that there is never a power cut and that there is food in abundance, even though she confesses that they have hardly any time to see each other and laugh as they used to. When Father Amadi writes, Kambili carries his letters around with her because she feels they make her confident and remind her of her worthiness.

When Kambili and Beatrice visit Jaja in prison once again, Kambili tries to make her brother feel better by promising him that in a week he will be released but she also senses that there is too much guilt hanging in his eyes. Meanwhile, Kambili is haunted with nightmares of shame and grief as well as of nightmares of the silence that pervaded their lives when Eugene was alive. Nonetheless, Kambili feels positive about their future and notices an equally positive change in Jaja when he comments on his mother's scarf since he had never bothered with what people would wear. Kambili comforts her mother by telling her that once Jaja is out of prison they will take him to Nsukka and go to America to visit their aunty and that Jaja will plant purple hibiscus like he used to. As Kambili laughs and succeeds in making her mother smile, she looks at the skies above and feels that 'the new rains will come down soon' as Amaka had promised.

Analysis – Epilogue (pages 295 to 307)

The last section, aptly entitled 'A Different Silence – The Present', is indeed written in the present tense throughout, so as to give the impression that what is being narrated by Kambili in writing is taking place contemporaneously.

Kambili starts by describing their way to prison and she notices how her mother does not bother with her appearance anymore, that she does not care if her wrapper comes loose and reveals any defects underneath. Beatrice does not care about how she looks and this is due to the fact that her son Jaja has been locked up because of what she has done; she could never forgive herself for her son's incarceration when it should have been herself in prison. She has in fact written many letters claiming her guilt and trying to prove her son's innocence, but all is in vain, because people think that she has gone mad by the strange twist of events.

Kambili then reveals that they are hoping that Jaja would be finally released from prison. After the Head of State's death and due to the fact that the old government had been blamed for killing Eugene, Jaja faces the possibility of being released. This does not mean, however, that it will be immediate – for some, it takes up to eight years – and even when he is released from prison after the thirty-one months he has spent there, he won't emerge unscathed by his stay and by the events that have ultimately shaped his future.

Kambili and her mother yearn for change, for a new beginning, craving for peace and hope. The fact that they cannot share such peace is because Beatrice has been shattered by all that she has experienced in her life; it might be late in the day for her to think about hope, because her guilt-ridden state of mind disallows her to be too positive. Kambili, on the other hand, has matured and, thanks to Father Amadi and Ifeoma's family, she has been led to believe in herself more and thus hope for a better and brighter future.

Yet, there are things that will be left unsaid, things that mother and daughter know about but would prefer to keep quiet about. It is very ironic because now that Eugene is not around anymore, they should not be afraid of voicing their opinions and yet, his presence still looms above their heads and they have learnt in time that there are moments in which certain things should be left unsaid. Kambili starts to be aware of her mother's depressive state – she does not talk anymore but simply sits and stares. In the meantime, Kambili yearns to go back to Nsukka, even though she doesn't know anybody there. She will always be indebted to Nsukka, for it is the place that has changed her life, it has given her a unknown kind of freedom.

Whilst Kambili witnesses her brother's degradation in prison and her mother's depression, she receives news from Ifeoma. Even though Ifeoma had faced poverty when at Nsukka, she would still prefer to be there rather than to have started from scratch in an unknown country where the foreigner is not considered equal to the native. Kambili feels that Ifeoma is nostalgic for the past and that she yearns for a brighter future that seems to be unreachable and hence does not linger on the present.

Kambili also recalls that Ifeoma had once told her how some people give up trying to rule themselves because they fail therefore they lose hope. This is very insightful but also very pessimistic because it shows that Ifeoma has shed her idealism and has had to accept the limitations that had been imposed on her by the country that she would have protected, the country she would have fought for. Amaka's letters seem to echo her mother's, as they are full of regret, sadness and nostalgia for their true home. Amaka thus feels the same way as her mother: despite the commodities and safety that living in America offers, the lifestyle there is so busy and jam-packed with food, things and activities that there is no time for them to enjoy one another's company; hence, without knowing, Amaka and her family long to return to their former way of life that has now been replaced by a more materialistic lifestyle.

Father Amadi also writes to Kambili from Germany, but his letters are more about her than about him; he is very ambiguous when Kambili asks him whether he is happy, preferring to answer that priesthood is his priority. This lessens the pain that she feels because of the absence of the people who care about her, and it also makes her stronger for when she has to visit her brother in prison. When Kambili and Beatrice go to see Jaja, she notices how quickly he is changing, not only physically but also in his attitude: he shrugs when they mention his eventual release, he talks about there being interesting characters in prison, even though his eyes had a hardened and unyielding expression.

What has not changed completely is Kambili and Jaja's ability to communicate by means of a glance, but now Kambili is afraid to look into her brother's eyes because she knows that he will hide what he feels and think badly about himself. This is due to the fact that Jaja feels guilty about not having done more to better their situation.

Whilst Jaja eats heartily to please his mother, Kambili feels that a different and more relieving kind of silence surrounded them. So the silence there is between them is not the threatening one that they experienced when Eugene was alive; it is a willed silence, one that allows them to enjoy one another's company without expecting too much, a kind of silence that however conceals certain things that Kambili would like to say.

As Kambili closes her narrative, she reassures her mother by telling her that when Jaja will be released from prison, they will go to America to visit Ifeoma, that they will plant purple hibiscus and that things will be good – it is the daughter who is trying to pacify the mother and make her happy and tranquil and this shows how much Kambili has matured throughout the novel and has achieved much more than she had bargained for. The novel's open-ended conclusion is laden with symbolism when Kambili tells the reader that they await the new rains. As one remembers what Papa-Nnukwu had said, that new rains bring change, thus Kambili ends her narrative by waiting for the new rains that could bring with them new hopes, new freedom, and a new life for her and her family.

Characters

Kambili Achike

Kambili Achike is the narrator of the story in *Purple Hibiscus* and also the central character. Kambili is younger than her brother Jaja. At fifteen, she is a devoted Catholic and obedient daughter. Even though she is intelligent and carefully observes what goes on around her in minute detail, she is very shy and self-disciplined, and only after having spent some time at Aunty Ifeoma's house does she start opening up. Kambili changes throughout the novel with the help and understanding of Aunty Ifeoma and Father Amadi. Her cousins also warm up to her, particularly after they understand what she had been going through back in Enugu. This shows why Kambili is so distraught when Ifeoma and her family as well as Father Amadi leave the country.

Eugene Achike

Eugene is Kambili's father. He is the domineering patriarch of the Achike family and demands that his wife and children follow a very strict pattern by not only adhering to the Catholic faith but also by performing their duties. In fact, Kambili and Jaja are given a schedule where every aspect of their daily routine is accounted for and every minute of the day is rigidly planned. A wealthy businessman, Eugene is a pillar of his community: he donates money to numerous causes and individuals, and he stands up to injustice through the publishing of the *Standard*. However, Eugene also tends to be violent when his family do not meet his expectations, and he ends up punishing them severely by beating them until they succumb to his regime.

Chukwuka "Jaja" Achike

Jaja is Kambili's brother. At seventeen, he is an intelligent and diligent young man who is easily dominated by his father during most of the novel. Ultimately, he turns out to be overtly defiant after having lived at Aunty Ifeoma's house. He realises that it is time that he and his family have to stand up for what is rightfully theirs. He openly challenges Eugene by not receiving communion on Palm Sunday. When his father is found dead, he claims responsibility for his mother's crime and spends almost three years in prison before being granted amnesty.

Beatrice Achike

Beatrice is a quiet and submissive wife in the Achike household for most of the novel. As Kambili and Jaja's mother, she represents the warm, loving figure in the home and deeply contrasts the tyrannical father. She is terribly passive until she realises that she cannot cope with her husband's behaviour and poisons him. She is thereafter overcome by guilt of having allowed her son to take the blame. Towards the end of the novel, however, there are some signs that she will get better, particularly with the impending release of her son.

Aunty Ifeoma

Aunty Ifeoma is Eugene's sister, and a mother of three strong and determined children. As a widow, she is quite capable of taking care of her family while working as a lecturer at the University of Nigeria. She strikes an imposing presence to those who meet her and as a tall, intelligent woman, she is not afraid to stand up to her brother, even though her financial struggles force her to ask for his help occasionally. However, her determination and resourcefulness allow her to provide a much happier environment for her children than does Eugene for his family.

Amaka

Ifeoma's only daughter, Amaka is almost a carbon copy of her mother. Apart from walking and talking like her, Amaka exhibits strength of character and a pressing determination to survive against the odds. Kambili is in awe of her for most of the time spent together and initially Amaka considers Kambili to be an arrogant snob. This is because she is very outspoken and confident in contrast to her shy cousin. Amaka is not very excited about going to America and still feels deeply nostalgic when she does leave.

Obiora

As the eldest son of Ifeoma, Obiora has taken up the role of the man of the house after his father's death. Jaja is in awe of the way his cousin balances his family on his head as Obiora is younger than Jaja. Like Amaka, Obiora is outspoken and mature beyond his years. He challenges Father Amadi on many occasions and at times takes certain views to heart and as a result, Ifeoma and Father Amadi have to reproach him.

Father Amadi

Father Amadi is a young attractive priest who visits Aunty Ifeoma and her family very often. In fact, Amaka and Obiora claim that they are his favourite family but the other families all express warmth towards the youthful Catholic priest. He is open-minded and tolerant of different religions and is a clear contrast to the other priests who, like Father Benedict, are extremely strict and prescriptive in their religious approach. Father Amadi's joviality and kind-hearted approach draws Kambili towards him and consequently she falls in love with him. He handles her infatuation very sensitively and explains to her in a compassionate and sensible manner that he is devoted to the church. Everyone feels saddened by his departure and the families feel they are losing not only a priest but also a dear friend.

Father Benedict

As a white Catholic priest who had arrived in Nigeria to convert the locals to Catholicism, Father Benedict is also very strict and intolerant of people who are not self-disciplined. He strongly contrasts with Father Amadi and while the people have a friendly relationship with the latter, they are quite afraid of Father Benedict. Eugene and Father Benedict work together very often, striving to keep the people from losing their religious self-discipline.

Papa-Nnukwu

Papa-Nnukwu is a 'traditionalist' and one of the few elders who refused to convert to the new religion. As a result of his decision, his son Eugene has forsaken him and severed all ties from him, demanding that his wife and children do the same. Ifeoma, however, does not abandon her father and takes him in during the last days of his life. At Nsukka, Kambili and Jaja get to know the grandfather they hardly met and discover that Papa-Nnukwu is after all kind-hearted and endearing. They have only known him as a 'heathen' but he is after all only a man who is devoted to his indigenous culture.

Themes and Motifs

Religion

The theme of religion is a central theme in *Purple Hibiscus* as this is what has lead Eugene, a Nigerian who has converted to Catholicism, to turn away from his father, Papa-Nnukwu, who has refused to convert to Catholicism and has remained faithful to the traditional Igbo religion. One also sees various parallels in terms of religious attitudes between the characters of Father Benedict and Eugene who are fervent Catholics, whilst Father Amadi and Ifeoma who are more open-minded Catholics.

Oppression

Oppression and tyranny is seen in both the social milieu as well as within the Achike family. *Purple Hibiscus* focuses on the Achike family and how Eugene's rigid control occasionally turns to physical violence at home but he is the person who is publicly seen as one who fights for freedom. On the other hand one can also see that the military leaders who are leading the country to a chaotic and desperate situation because of their excessive control and greed. However, oppression leads to rebellion from those who are forced to be submissive and this is seen in both the public and the private scenes.

Freedom

Freedom is given pride of place in *Purple Hibiscus* as it is presented as something precious and it is associated with the character of Aunty Ifeoma. Ifeoma is a strong character who gives the weaker characters such as Beatrice, Jaja and Kambili hope for a better and brighter future and she helps and guides them in their pursuit of freedom. It is through Ifeoma that characters such as Jaja and Beatrice find the courage to break the silence and find freedom. The purple hibiscus plant which is rare and well tended by Ifeoma is also a symbol of freedom as presented in the novel.

Family and the role of the father

The reader is exposed to two very different families in *Purple Hibiscus*, that is, Eugene's family as well as Ifeoma's family. Eugene's family is an extremely quiet family and the members of this family shy away from talking freely for fear of angering Eugene and provoking his violent behaviour. On the other hand, Ifeoma is a widow who finds it hard to make ends meet and she has to raise three children on her own. Notwithstanding all of these difficulties, she still maintains a positive atmosphere at home which is characterised by laughter, communication, freedom and a strong sense of family.

Symbolism

Purple Hibiscus is full of various symbols the most significant of which is the purple hibiscus plant which represents the freedom that the various characters, in both the private as well as public spheres, strive for. Kambili also has various dreams throughout the novel which echo her thoughts and emotions and are symbolic in their own way. In addition certain objects such as the figurines, the missal and Beatrice's T-shirt are also representative of underlying issues, whilst the weather, the section titles and the author's use of colour also contribute to making this a highly intricate novel.

Daniela Muscat and Stephanie Xerri Aguis are both masters graduates and they have been teaching English for quite a number of years. Both Daniela Muscat and Stephanie Xerri Aguis teach English at Giovanni Curmi Higher Secondary School, Malta.